Animal Rights

Look for these and other books in the Lucent
Overview series:

Acid Rain
AIDS
Animal Rights
The Beginning of Writing
Dealing with Death
Drugs and Sports
Drug Trafficking
Endangered Species
Garbage
Homeless Children
The Olympic Games
Population
Smoking
Soviet-American Relations
Special Effects in the Movies
Teen Alcoholism
The UFO Challenge
Vietnam

Animal Rights

by Sunni Bloyd

LUCENT
B·O·O·K·S

Library of Congress Cataloging-in-Publication Data

Bloyd, Sunni.
    Animal rights / by Sunni Bloyd.
        p.   cm. — (Overview series)
    Includes bibliographical references.
    Summary: Discusses current animal-rights issues, their underlying
philosophies, and ways we can help curb animal abuse.
    ISBN 1-56006-114-6
    1. Animal rights—Juvenile literature.   [1. Animal rights
2. Animal welfare.]   I. Title.   II. Series: Lucent overview series.
HV4708.B58   1990
179'.3—dc20
                                               90-6197
                                                  CIP
                                                     AC

© Copyright 1990 by Lucent Books, Inc.
P.O. Box 289011, San Diego, CA 92198-0011

To my family: John R., A.C., and Jeremy, who cried when he learned that all the dinosaurs were dead.

Acknowledgements

The author would like to express her appreciation to those who provided assistance and information during the preparation of this book:

Leesuh Allen, Farm Animal Reform Movement; Linda Fuller; Marilyn Bates; Bill Andrews, California State Department of Education; Rosalina Hewiston, National Association of Biology Teachers; Marsha Kelly, National Board of Fur Farm Organizations; Julie Dunlap, the Humane Society of the United States; Ralston Purina Company; the American Heart Association; The Vegetarian Resource Group; The American Anti-Vivisection Society; The National Anti-Vivisection Society; *The Animals' Voice* Magazine; Animal Welfare Institute; The Humane Farming Association; People for the Ethical Treatment of Animals; Steve Kopperud, Animal Industry Foundation; Betty Denny Smith and Betsy K. Tyus, American Humane Association; ASPCA; Patti Finch, National Association for Environmental Education; Dr. Temple Grandon; Melissa Metzler, Professional Rodeo Cowboys Association; Debby Duel; Julie Van Ness, Argus Archives; Dr. Elliot Katz, In Defense of Animals; Susan La Chapelle, Maurine Aschoff, Sandy Cooper, and Jean Thompson, Villa Park Library; and Carol O'Sullivan.

Contents

Introduction

FOR CENTURIES HUMANS have made use of other species to meet their needs for food, clothing, transportation, sport, companionship, medical research, and entertainment.

But people's attitudes toward animals have gradually changed over time. Until the eighteenth century, for example, an animal was considered a piece of property, like a chair or a pair of shoes. There were no animal-protection laws. There was no punishment for causing an animal to suffer, and an animal's owner could beat, starve, or even kill it without interference. Now many organizations have been formed to protect animals. These organizations break into two distinct groups with different goals—animal welfare and animal rights.

The first animal welfare organizations were formed in England 160 years ago to encourage the humane treatment of animals. Members of these groups believed that people ought to avoid making animals suffer unnecessarily. They believed in protecting animals from cruelty.

Today, these organizations include the American Humane Society, the American Society for the Prevention of Cruelty to Animals (ASPCA), and the National Anti-Vivisection Society (NAVS). These organizations investigate reports of animal abuse in places such as public riding stables, traveling animal shows, or private homes and businesses. They

(opposite page) Animal welfare and animal rights groups try to protect animals from human cruelty. Members of some of these groups marched in Washington, D.C. in June, 1990, to show their opposition to the use of animals in medical research.

Animal rights activists protested the treatment of animals at the University of Pennsylvania Veterinary School.

work with the government to develop new anticruelty laws and help enforce old ones. They also educate the public about animal abuse through advertising and publications.

Animal rights organizations, first appeared in Great Britain during the 1970s. These groups' goals and practices are more aggressive than those of the animal welfare organizations. Members of animal rights organizations believe that the needs of animals are just as important as the needs of humans. Their goals range from securing the right to kind treatment for animals to abolishing animal experimentation and stopping people from raising animals for food.

Conservative animal rights groups, such as People for the Ethical Treatment of Animals (PETA) and the Farm Animal Reform Movement (FARM), try to stop practices they consider immoral and inhumane. For example, FARM is leading the fight to abolish the practice of keeping veal calves in small cages where they cannot move or turn around. These groups use demonstrations and public pressure to force stores, manufacturers, researchers, and government agencies to change policies that harm animals.

Nonpolitical protest

A few radical animal rights groups, such as the Animal Liberation Front (ALF) and the Band of Mercy, believe that extreme steps must be taken to get their point across. These small, secret bands conduct night raids on laboratories, seizing research animals and destroying records. Some groups also raid factory farms. Once ALF claimed to have poisoned bars of candy produced by a British manufacturer that conducted animal testing.

Members of these groups justify vandalism and the destruction of private property by claiming their actions save animals' lives. They reject the tactics

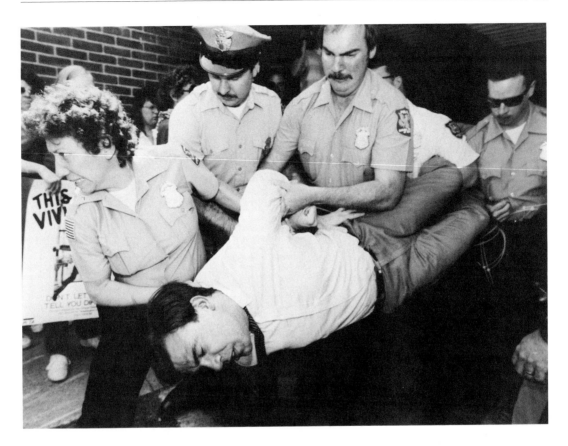

A member of People for the Ethical Treatment of Animals was arrested during protests at the National Institutes of Health in Maryland. Group members were protesting experimentation on animals.

of political action and demonstrations used by other groups. Animal liberationists believe that the only way to end animal research is to cause so much damage that laboratories are forced to close.

Animal welfare advocates, animal rights activists, and animal liberationists share many of the same goals, although the means they use to achieve these goals differ. All of these groups believe that animals have a right to life without suffering or early death.

What are animal rights?

How can an animal have rights? To understand this, we must first look at the meaning of the word *right*. A right is a claim to something. Human rights, such as the right to a free press or the right to have private property, are based in tradition, morality, and

A Pennsylvania poultry farmer uses fans and insulation to protect her broiler hens from the heat.

the law. Our rights may be ignored or violated by others, but they continue to exist because they are part of a commonly accepted standard of how people ought to be treated.

Peter Singer, an Australian professor of philosophy, believes that animals should also be guaranteed certain rights.

Animal rights activists agree with Singer and want these animal rights to be guaranteed by law. They believe that animals have three basic rights:

1. Each species has the right to express the natural behaviors of its kind. Every animal has behaviors that are natural to it. For example, calves have an urge to chew their cud, partially digested grass or hay. Chickens need to peck and scratch for their food. Animal rights advocates want to stop any human practice, such as feeding veal calves only liquid formula or raising chickens in cages high above the ground, that interferes with these behaviors.

2. All animals have the right to a natural life span without suffering neglect or cruelty. Current animal welfare laws protect many animals from neglect and cruelty. Animal rights advocates want to expand the definition of cruelty to include fear, suffering, or early death caused by humans. This is perhaps the most controversial idea of all because to respect this right, people must not eat meat, hunt, conduct experiments on animals, or wear clothes made from animal products.

3. Every animal has the right to a humane death. Some activists think animals should not be killed for any reason. These people even oppose the humane killing of animals suffering from incurable illnesses. Animal rights advocates do believe, how-

Animal rights activists protest the practice of feeding liquid formula to calves that will be slaughtered and sold for veal.

ever, that when animals are killed, whether they are put to sleep, slaughtered for food, or killed during scientific experiments, death should be as painless and free of fear as possible.

But not everyone believes animals should have these three rights.

Most medical researchers, animal trainers, and farmers believe that animals do not have the same rights that people claim. While these people think we ought to treat animals humanely, they also think we should be able to use them as we wish.

Supporters of this point of view argue that humans have always used animals to satisfy their needs. They contend that most animals benefit from their relationship with humans and would suffer without it. As proof, they point to the fact that most animals in the care of humans are healthier, better fed, and safer than those in the wild. In addition, many animals even seem to enjoy being with people.

Most people believe that animals, such as this mother pig and her piglets, should be treated humanely even when they are used for food, clothing, or medical research.

With so many different opinions, the animal rights debate is confusing. Ultimately, each individual must alone decide what to believe. But it is important to understand the arguments on both sides to be able to develop an informed and reasonable opinion.

In the end, perhaps the controversy will help animals no matter what conclusions are reached. For everyone agrees about one aspect of animal rights: only concerned human beings can improve the conditions in which animals live.

1

Do Animals Have Rights?

THE DEBATE OVER animal rights has its roots in the beliefs of previous generations. Judeo-Christian religious thought, Greek philosophy, the scientific theories of the French philosopher Descartes, and eighteenth-century social reforms in England have contributed ideas to both sides of the argument. It is important to understand these early beliefs because they continue to influence contemporary thinking about the role and value of animals in human society.

Beliefs about human superiority

Two of the earliest influences on the way people think about animals were the teachings of the Judeo-Christian religion and of the Greek philosophers. Both schools of thought advanced the idea that human beings are superior to other species.

Early Judeo-Christian religious teachings placed people above animals in the hierarchy of creatures. The Old Testament outlines this philosophy in Gen. 1: "Then God said, 'Let us make man in our image and likeness to rule the fish of the sea, the birds of heaven, the cattle, all wild animals on earth, and all reptiles that crawl upon the earth.'"

(opposite page) Many people find comfort and companionship with their pets.

17

Although the Old Testament says God gave humans power over animals, it condemns treating animals badly. Jews and Christians are instructed to take good care of their animals. "A righteous man cares for his beast but a wicked man is cruel at heart," according to Prov. 12.

The ancient Greeks also believed that humans were superior to animals, and they singled out the human ability to reason as proof. According to this idea, each person has a "rational soul," an immortal or undying spiritual element that enables people to choose between right and wrong thus. The Greeks argued that animals cannot reason because they lack souls.

Aristotle, a third century B.C. philosopher, expanded this idea. He placed animals at the bottom of an imaginary pyramid of ability. Aristotle thought superior people belonged at the top of the pyramid as rulers. Beneath them came less intelligent or talented people. According to Aristotle, they deserved to be slaves. Animals ranked below the slaves because they could not think rationally.

Aristotle said people have the right to own and use animals as they wish because they are inferior to people, but he thought cruelty to animals was wrong. Being cruel was wrong because it causes a human's rational soul to become harsh and insensitive.

God made mankind superior

Later, these ideas became an important element of modern Christian belief. For many Christians, the theory that only humans have souls justified the Old Testament passages that said God had given humankind dominance over other living creatures. So, Christians believed that God had intended for humans to use animals as they wished.

Until the seventeenth century, religious belief controlled science and philosophy. Scientists were punished if their ideas deviated from accepted religious thought. For example, in 1633 the astronomer Galileo barely escaped being burned at the stake for saying that the earth moved around the sun. This idea contradicted the prevailing theory that God had made the earth the center of the universe.

The scientific method

But a revolution took place in Western thought during the seventeenth century. Science began to emerge and separate from religion. A number of brilliant scientists and philosophers established the idea that scientific conclusions must be based on provable facts. To this day, the majority of scientists believe that emotions and beliefs interfere with the discovery of knowledge.

The pattern for early scientific investigation using animals was set by the French philosopher and mathematician René Descartes. Descartes recognized that the universe was controlled by scientific laws. He thought these laws caused everything, including living creatures, to operate mechanically, like clocks. Anything from the movement of the moon around the earth to the digestion of food inside the stomach could be explained by scientific laws.

Descartes's theory revealed similarities between animals and humans. Both humans and animals had hearts, stomachs, and lungs, for example. But Descartes still did not believe animals could experience thought, emotion, or the sensations of pain and pleasure. He believed that only humans are able to think and feel because they have souls. Animals, he argued, were merely living robots, able to move but without consciousness or feelings because they do not have souls. The idea that animals did not feel pain was accepted by most scientists.

At the time, scientific knowledge of physiology and human anatomy was limited. Because the dissection of human corpses or painful experiments on humans were forbidden by religious authorities, little was known about the organs of the body or how they operate. But there was no law against experimenting on living animals, a process called vivisection. So, Descartes and other scientists began to vivisect animals in search of more knowledge about physiology.

The theories of Descartes inspired a craze for biological experimentation that swept Europe during the seventeenth century. Philosophers, ambassadors, doctors, members of royalty, and even fashionable ladies attended public demonstrations of vivisection and conducted experiments themselves.

Because of the limited scientific knowledge of the time, most experiments were poorly planned and executed. In addition, few scientists actually did ex-

Early seventeenth-century scientists, like Galileo, were persecuted for their work. But an emerging separation between religion and science fostered development of new scientific laws.

periments for a specific purpose. They were more likely to experiment because they were curious. When experimenting on animals, self-taught scientists in search of knowledge felt free to cut, burn, poison, and kill animals.

In 1664, Samuel Pepys, an Englishman who witnessed and then described many of the important events of the time in his diary, wrote about an attempt to kill a dog by injecting opium into a vein. "[The experimenters] did fail mightily in hitting the vein and in effect did not do the business after so many trials. But with the little they got in, the dog did presently fall asleep, and so lay till we cut him up."

Other experimenters electrocuted dogs, suffocated mice by putting them in jars and removing all the air, amputated horses' hooves, and nailed dogs and cats to the wall before vivisecting them. In one case, a dog remained conscious while its stomach was removed, then sewn back into place upside down.

This hit-or-miss approach to animal experimentation produced much unrecognized pain and suffering in its animal subjects. Some important advances, however, were made. For example, the English doctor William Harvey discovered circulation by dissecting live deer. He proved that the heart pumps blood through the body.

Similar responses

Ironically, it was these cruel experiments that made people question Descartes's theory. Vivisection revealed many more similarities between the biological systems of humans and animals—especially the nervous systems, which are responsible for the sensations of touch, taste, smell, and pain. Furthermore, vivisection revealed that animals responded to pain in a similar way to humans. By the last half of the eighteenth century, most experimenters became

English physician William Harvey discovered how blood circulates through the body by dissecting live deer. Here, Harvey demonstrates his discovery for King Charles I.

convinced that animals must experience pain.

While this realization did not necessarily change scientists' opinions about animals, reforms in the way animal experiments were conducted did take place. People interested in biological sciences formed organizations that reported the results of their experiments to other scientists. Gradually, they refined experimental techniques and developed standards for research that lessened the suffering of experimental animals.

It is difficult today to understand the insensitivity to animal suffering and pain that was common all over Europe until the end of the eighteenth century. One reason people cared so little about animals was that their own lives were short, violent, and full of disease. People were so busy simply trying to keep alive, it seemed like a luxury to care about animals. Favorite pastimes included attending public hangings and watching performers at local fairs eat live cats for a fee. Coachmen freely beat their horses to death in public streets. If bystanders objected, they were told to mind their own business.

Reform in England

Yet by the end of the century, attitudes in England had begun to change. An emphasis on sensitivity and kindness, called humanitarianism, gradually turned people away from the harsh ideas of the past and encouraged them to address such issues as slavery, prison reform, child welfare, and care of the insane.

Poets, clergymen, writers, philosophers, and even a few sportsmen condemned the cruel treatment of animals that they saw all around them. For example, English author Samuel Johnson attacked fox hunters for harassing what he called a "small inedible British beast" with horses, hounds, and spades. Author James Thompson spent a Sunday afternoon thinking about the captive birds and wild animals in London's Regents Zoo Park. "Oh, how they must suffer!" he cried out.

The humanitarians gave many reasons for treating animals kindly. All of these reasons were based on the idea that humans are superior to animals. Some thought that cruelty to animals is bad because it leads to cruelty to humans. Religious people took the Judeo-Christian point of view that animal abuse is mismanagement of a resource God has given mankind.

Jeremy Bentham, an English philosopher writing toward the end of the eighteenth century, was the first to claim that animals had rights, and his ideas on the subject are still quoted by animal rights activists today. Bentham theorized that the only real evil in the

English philosopher Jeremy Bentham was one of the first people to publicly claim that animals had rights.

world is suffering, and the only real good is pleasure. Anything that causes pain must be bad, and anything that causes pleasure must be good. Since animals can feel both pain and pleasure, Bentham reasoned, they should have the same rights to pleasure and freedom from suffering that humans do.

Animal rights legislation

In 1821, Richard Martin, an Irish member of the British Parliament, took up the cause of animal rights. His efforts on behalf of animals earned Martin the nickname of "Humanity." First, he proposed a bill forbidding the mistreatment of horses. Other members of Parliament regarded it as a joke. "He'll be legislating for dogs next!" someone quipped. Before the laughter died away, somebody else provoked a fresh burst of merriment by adding, "And cats!" With this kind of attitude displayed by other lawmakers, the bill promptly failed.

One year later, Martin tried again. This time he proposed to make it a crime to "wantonly and cruelly beat, abuse, or ill-treat any horse, mare, gelding, mule, ass, ox, cow, heifer, steer, sheep or other cattle" belonging to another person. Martin's bill became law in 1822.

Martin's Act, as the new law was known, was the first law in England to make animal abuse a crime. Although Martin's Act did not apply to all animals, it set a precedent for later laws.

Passage of an animal welfare act did not mean that the law would be enforced, however. British authorities were not interested in investigating or prosecuting animal abuse cases. So Martin himself gathered evidence and prosecuted cruel coachmen and cart drivers. Yet he could not do the job alone. Martin and a number of other humanitarians decided an animal welfare organization would be necessary to enforce the law.

In 1824, Martin formed the Society for the Prevention of Cruelty to Animals, an English animal welfare organization now known as the Royal Society for the Prevention of Cruelty to Animals (RSPCA). The RSPCA had two purposes: to see that cases of abuse were prosecuted in a court of law and to teach the British public about cruelty to animals. In its first year, the society successfully brought nearly 150 cases of animal abuse to trial.

The ideas of the English reformers spread to other countries, including the United States. An American diplomat in England named Henry Bergh was inspired by a visit to the RSPCA. After returning to the United States, Bergh began the first American animal welfare organization in 1861. It was known as the American Society for the Prevention of Cruelty to Animals (ASPCA). The ASPCA and other organizations like it still help make and enforce anti-cruelty laws in the United States.

Charles Darwin

In 1858, a scientist named Charles Darwin proposed a theory that further changed the way people think about animals. Darwin's theory of evolution states that all plants and animals have evolved, or developed, from earlier life forms. According to this theory, even humans are the descendants of animals and share common ancestors with the apes.

Darwin compared animals and humans and concluded that "the senses and intuitions, the various emotions. . .such as love, memory, attention, and curiosity, imitation, reason, etc., of which man boasts, may be found in [developing] or even sometimes in a well-developed condition, in the lower animals." Even human morality was descended from animal traits, Darwin said, because animals enjoy one another's company, feel sympathy for each other, and help each other.

Darwin's ideas shocked many people because they seemed to contradict the Christian belief that humans

Charles Darwin theorized that human beings evolved from animals, an idea that shocked many people of the time and continues to be controversial.

Bobo the dog received a mechanical heart in experiments leading to the first artificial heart transplants in humans. Some people say human beings should not use animals for these kinds of experiments.

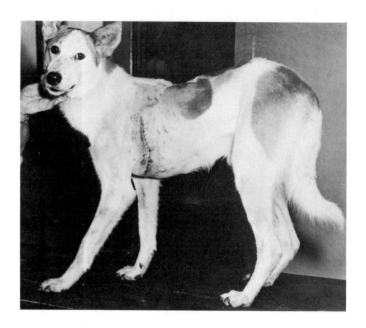

had been originally created in a form superior to and different from other living creatures. Over the next thirty years, however, studies comparing animal and human physiology confirmed Darwin's theories. Scientists and educated people began to accept the idea that humans are animals, too.

Although controversial, the idea that humans are descended from animal ancestors has now gained wide acceptance. Many people interpret evolutionary theory to mean that humanity does not have a God-given right to dominate other species, since humans are not very different from animals. This belief eventually became the basis of the animal rights movement.

Animal welfare or animal rights?

For more than a century after Darwin, the treatment of animals gradually improved as animal welfare organizations educated the public about animal abuse and as better animal protection laws were enacted. However, even those who were concerned with animal welfare still believed in the superiority of the human species and its right to use animals to meet human needs.

In 1975 Peter Singer wrote a book that challenged these beliefs. His book, *Animal Liberation: A New Ethics for Our Treatment of Animals,* has been called the bible of the animal rights movement. In it, Singer argues that vivisection exploits animals. He compares such practices to slavery because they use animals to satisfy human needs but ignore the needs of the animals themselves. Never before had anyone questioned the right of humans to use animals for these things.

Singer created a new word, *speciesism,* to describe the way humans view animals. According to Singer, speciesism is the belief that humans are better than other species. Humans who do something to an animal that they would not do to a person are guilty of speciesism.

Singer's ideas go a step further than old ideas

Members of People for the Ethical Treatment of Animals don monkey masks and prison stripes in a protest at the U.S. Department of Health and Human Services.

Animal rights activists believe chickens suffer when they are packed in crates like these where they cannot move or see sunlight.

about animal welfare. Singer believes animals should be liberated from exploitation. He claims that all beings that can feel pain or emotion should have some basic rights. They should be able to live a natural life free from human exploitation, without unnecessary pain, suffering, or fear of early death.

Singer condemns factory farming, animal experimentation, and similar uses of animals because they cause animal suffering. He believes that chickens, calves, pigs, and other animals suffer when kept confined indoors in small cages or crates where they cannot move around or see the sun. Similar conditions in animal research centers make life miserable for experimental animals, according to Singer. In addition, many common procedures, such as feeding rats large doses of harmful chemicals in animal research, are very painful. Singer claims that many animals die unnecessarily as a result of the stress and disease they experience under these conditions.

Singer feels that one important way to stop animal exploitation is to stop killing them for food, and he urges people who are concerned about animals to become vegetarians. A vegetarian himself, Singer believes that the whole process of raising animals for food and slaughtering them is immoral because it causes them great suffering.

How should humans treat animals?

Singer's ideas have influenced a large minority of people around the world. Animal rights groups are active in Germany, Australia, Great Britain, Canada, and the United States, to name only a few locations. In some places they have come into conflict with animal welfare organizations that endorse activities, such as animal research and animal training, that animal rights groups disapprove of.

Although the animal rights movement condemns some of the ways people use animals, it accepts many of the traditional relationships between humans and animals, such as the bond between pet and owner. Perhaps these relationships will also change as people become more sensitive to the needs of other living beings.

Animal rights activists believe that many animals, such as cows in this feedlot, suffer from inhumane living conditions.

2

Animal Research

BIOMEDICAL RESEARCH is research conducted on living creatures to determine how their bodies operate or how to treat illnesses and accidents. Many important medical advances have come from this kind of experimentation, which most often uses animal subjects. Since 1901, fifty-seven Nobel Prizes have been awarded to scientists whose work was based, at least in part, on animal research.

Animal research has made possible the vaccines against polio, mumps, measles, rubella, and smallpox. It has played a vital role in the development of lifesaving techniques such as open-heart surgery, microsurgery to reattach limbs, and organ transplants. Other medical advances that came from animal research include the use of insulin to control diabetes and the development of drugs important in the treatment of asthma, alcoholism, arthritis, ulcers, and high blood pressure. Frankie J. Trull, president of the Foundation for Biomedical Research, claims, "It is safe to say that, if you are an American alive today, you most likely have benefited from animal research."

Yet antivivisectionist groups like People for the Ethical Treatment of Animals claim that animal testing is inhumane and campaign to end or restrict it. PETA and other groups use direct mail campaigns and public protest to inspire others to end animal re-

(opposite page) Some vaccines for humans are created by infecting animals with a mild form of a disease. Here, chicken embryos are inoculated with doses of a virus.

31

Approximately sixty-one thousand monkeys and apes were used for medical research in 1987 in the United States. This monkey is part of research done by the Primate Laboratory at the University of Wisconsin.

search. As a result, in the past few years Congress has received more mail on the subject of animal research than any other topic. Dr. Charles McCarthy, head of the Office for Protection from Research Risks at the National Institutes of Health (NIH), reports that the mail response is one hundred people against animal research for every person in favor of it. Because the use of animals in research is so controversial, it is necessary to learn more about how and why these animals are used before taking sides.

How animals are used in research

According to the U.S. Office of Technology Assessment, the 1,260 registered research laboratories in the United States use between seventeen and twenty-two million animals each year. About 90 percent of these are rats, mice, and other rodents. In 1987, other animals used in research totaled approximately 180,000 dogs, 50,000 cats, 61,000 nonhuman primates (monkeys and apes), 530,000 guinea pigs, and 554,385 rabbits. Ten federal agencies, including the Departments of Agriculture, Defense, Energy, Interior, and Transportation, sponsor or conduct lab tests with animals.

When most people think of animal research, they imagine animals being used in the development of new drugs and medical techniques. While this is an important part of animal research, animals are also used in medical experiments in many other ways.

For example, products such as estrogen, an important ingredient in birth control pills, and insulin, used to treat diabetes, are extracted from the blood, urine, or organs of animals. Certain vaccines are created by infecting animals with a mild form of the disease. These vaccines are then processed for human use. For example, the smallpox vaccine is produced on the skins of calves or sheep. Other animals are used to diagnose serious illnesses in humans, including anthrax and syphilis. Frogs or rabbits are injected with material from a sick person's blood, then the doctor analyzes the changes within the animal. Toxicity testing exposes animals to chemicals to determine whether they are safe for human use or to determine the safe limits of use for chemicals that are known to be dangerous. Finally, psychologists use animal subjects to study behaviors as varied as learning, parenting, and aggression.

Not all research is harmful to animals. In a 1985 survey, the Department of Agriculture found that 62 percent of experiments using animal subjects involve no pain for the animals. In another 32 percent of the studies, the animals feel no pain because they receive anesthesia or painkillers. In only 6 percent of the studies do animals experience pain. In these studies, drugs or other treatment to numb pain must be withheld because they would affect the results of the experiment.

Laws that protect research animals

To ensure that laboratory animals receive humane handling and housing, two federal laws have set standards: the U.S. Animal Welfare Act and the

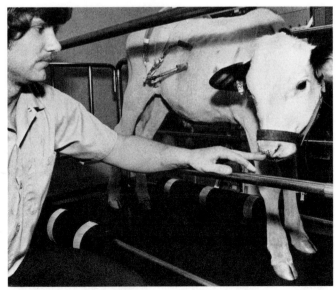

A technician examines this three-month-old calf three weeks after it received an artificial heart.

Animals used for research in 1986 and some of the benefits—		
	Primates 49,000	AIDS research, vaccine development, studies of Alzheimer's and Parkinson's diseases
	Cats 54,000	Vision research
	Dogs 180,000	Heart-surgery research
	Rats, mice 12-15 mil.	Cancer research, safety testing of new drugs
USN&WR—Basic data: U.S. Dept. of Agriculture, Office of Technology Assessment		

Health Research Extension Act of 1985.

The U.S. Animal Welfare Act (AWA) was passed in 1966 and amended in 1970, 1976, and 1985. It is enforced by the U.S. Department of Agriculture. The AWA requires animal dealers to be licensed, establishes review committees to approve planned animal experiments, and regulates the transportation of animals to be used in laboratories. The animals covered by this act include dogs, cats, apes, monkeys, lemurs, rabbits, hamsters, and guinea pigs.

The 1985 amendment to the AWA requires scientists using animals for research in a licensed research center to submit a detailed plan of their experiment, called a protocol, to an animal-use committee for approval. The protocol explains why animals must be used, what kind of animals they will be, how many will be needed, how they will be housed, exactly what will be done to each animal, and what painkillers will be used if they are necessary. If the protocol calls for painful procedures without painkillers, the researcher must explain why it is not appropriate to use them. For example, sometimes painkillers change the effects of other drugs, and this interference could invalidate an experiment. Animals that will suffer as a result of an experiment must be euthanatized, or painlessly killed, before the animals awaken from the anesthesia.

This law (protecting animals) is limited, however. Approximately 70 percent of the animals used in research are not covered. This is because AWA does not apply to farm animals, rats, mice, birds, and cold-blooded animals like snakes and lizards.

The second federal law that regulates the use and care of lab animals is the Health Research Extension Act of 1985. It applies only to research facilities that receive federal funds. Under this act, the secretary of health and human services establishes guidelines for the proper care and treatment of research animals. Known as the "Public Health Service Policy on Human Care and Use of Laboratory Animals," these guidelines are similar to the regulations of AWA. The Public Health Service can withhold federal funds from research facilities that do not comply with its guidelines.

Why animals are used in research

Scientists say that biomedical research must be conducted on living animals for several reasons. Researchers Alan M. Goldberg and John M. Frazier are two of many scientists who argue that there are no effective substitutes for animal research.

Animals are useful in research because they are similar to humans in many ways. Cats, for instance, are used in research to discover more about the human liver, middle ear and eardrum, and skin. Dogs and nonhuman primates, such as apes and monkeys, are also used in this type of research. Information gained from studies on these animals has a good chance of providing doctors with knowledge they can apply to the problems humans have with similar diseases.

Finally, animals take the place of people in dangerous or painful experiments. This is particularly important when testing new drugs or surgery. "The

Research on cats has provided valuable information on the human liver, middle ear and eardrum, and skin. Researchers at the University of Pennsylvania implanted an electrode in the head of this cat.

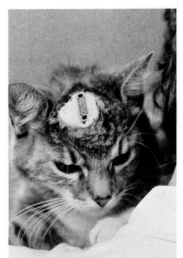

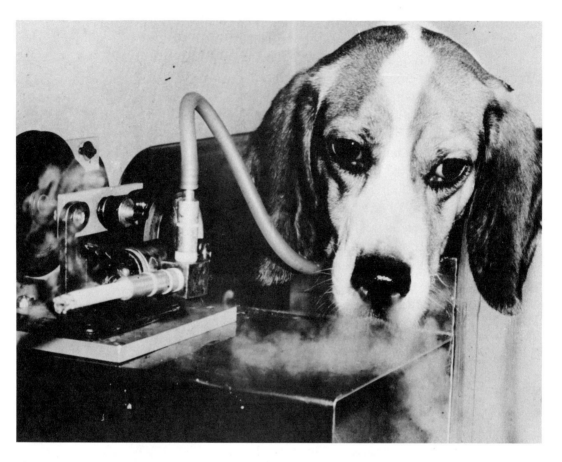

This beagle is one of ten dogs used in research on the link between smoking and emphysema, a disease that destroys lung tissue. The machine at the left pumps cigarette smoke directly into the dog's windpipe through a plastic tube.

only alternative—releasing a drug without such testing—amounts to *human* experimentation," says author Timothy Noah.

It is generally agreed throughout the world today that it is wrong to experiment on humans. This agreement was formalized in the Declaration of Helsinki in 1965. According to this agreement, which has been signed by most of the nations of the world, researchers must obtain the permission of an ethics committee before they conduct experiments with humans.

Ethics committees try to make sure that an experiment will not harm the patients that take part in it. Usually, they require that a new drug has been proven safe on animals before it is given to people.

This rule is not strictly enforced if the drug contains ingredients that are believed to be safe, the drug is extremely valuable, or the people who will be taking it have only a short time to live. The drug AZT, for example, was given to AIDS patients before the testing process in animals was completed. The patients were willing to take AZT because there was a chance the drug could halt the progression of their disease.

How valuable is animal research?

Some of the strongest supporters of biomedical research are those who have learned the value of it through personal experience. Judy Jaffee is one such supporter. Her daughter Gail developed Crohn's disease (an intestinal condition that makes digesting food very difficult) in 1981 at the age of seven. Malnutrition resulting from the disease stunted Gail's growth. She spent several years in and out of hospitals, undergoing intravenous feedings, operations, and other treatments as doctors tried to stop the progress of the disease.

"I remember my child looking at me and asking me if she was going to die," Judy Jaffee recalled. "I was able to look her in the eye and tell her truthfully that she would live because of medical techniques that came about from experiments on animals."

Gail did live, and today her disease is in remission. All of the treatments that saved her life were developed through years of animal experimentation.

"If the animal activists succeed in impeding research, the development of new cures and treatments will decline," predicts Steve Carroll, executive director of Incurably Ill for Animal Research. "Millions of Americans will suffer."

While animal rights advocates admit that animal research has resulted in some benefits to human health, they insist that it is inhumane and no longer necessary. "Animal testing is one of the most wasteful and incredibly cumbersome methodologies in

"I've been asked to test some stupid things in my time . . ."

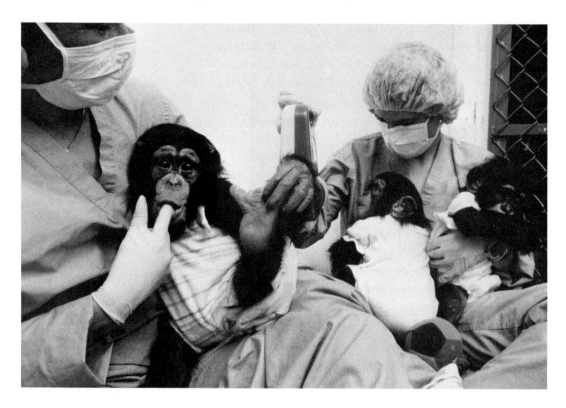

Many facilities that use animals in experiments pride themselves on humane treatment. The primate lab at New York University is considered a model for its treatment of its chimps.

science today," says Dr. Neal Barnard, psychiatrist and president of the Physicians Committee for Responsible Medicine.

"There have been some medical advances, of course," admits activist George Cave, "but the payoff is slight. When you're doing billions of animal experiments, it would be a miracle if there weren't some developments."

While animal welfare organizations work to reduce the number of animals used in testing and to eliminate the pain they suffer, animal rights activists want a total end to animal research. "It's not better cages we work for, but empty cages," says Tom Regan, a leader of the movement. "We want every animal out." Animal rights activists not only question the usefulness of animal experimentation but also believe such experiments are cruel and inhumanely conducted.

Are animals treated inhumanely in research labs? Two widely publicized cases of alleged cruelty to animals during the 1980s focused national attention on the question and gave new life to the animal rights movement.

In 1981, an undercover activist named Alex Pacheco documented conditions in a lab at the Institute for Behavioral Research in Silver Springs, Maryland. The research was to determine proper treatment for stroke victims and involved cutting nerves in monkeys' arms and legs, then trying to teach them to use the limbs again. Left unattended, the monkeys often chewed off their fingers because they could not feel them. Pacheco, who later founded PETA, filed animal cruelty charges against Edward Taub, the director of the project.

A police raid seized seventeen apes and monkeys, many of them with surgically handicapped limbs. Taub was arrested and tried under cruelty laws. He was found guilty of neglecting the monkeys, but the judgment was later overturned. The National Institutes of Health cancelled his $221,000 grant. This was the first time in history that federally funded

"We're putting miners down the mine shaft to make sure it's safe for canaries . . ."

A researcher discusses the damage done by an activist group that ransacked a University of Pennsylvania laboratory that was doing head injury research.

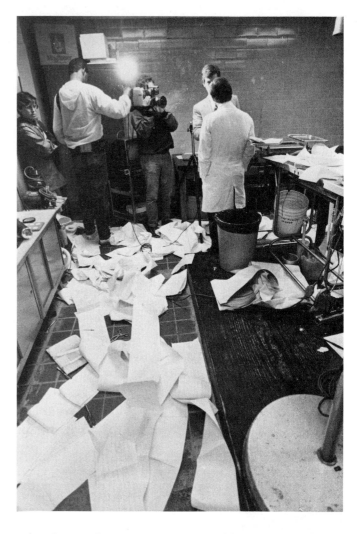

animal experiments were stopped because of public protests.

Another famous case took place in 1983 at the University of Pennsylvania Head Injury Clinical Research Center. In this case, monkeys had been given head injuries during experiments that were part of a research project aimed at improving treatment for human accident victims. A group of Animal Liberation Front members seized several dozen videotapes that graphically illustrated the experiments conducted at the clinic. ALF gave the tapes to

PETA, which released them in the form of a movie called *Unnecessary Fuss*.

The videotapes, never intended to be seen by the public, shocked those who saw them. They showed the experimenters making fun of the monkeys they had crippled, reusing surgical tools that fell on the floor, and smoking during surgery. Particularly upsetting was the process researchers used to cause the monkeys' head injuries. Monkeys wore cement helmets while given a blow to the head by a hydraulic jack. Removing the helmet required as many as 160 blows with hammers and screwdrivers, while the experimental animal remained conscious throughout the entire ordeal. In one portion of the videotape, a researcher could be heard saying, "Let's hope the antivivisectionists never get ahold of this."

Repercussions

Federal funding to the research center was cut by the Department of Health and Human Services following national screenings of the videotape. The research center was eventually closed.

These cases attracted national attention. Congressional hearings investigated how NIH, which had funded the Silver Springs project, and the U.S. Department of Agriculture which had inspected it, could have overlooked such conditions. In 1985, Congress amended AWA to include stricter standards for animal welfare. Many of the provisions enacted in 1985—such as a requirement to provide exercise areas for dogs and take other steps to "promote the psychological well-being" of primates —have not yet been put into effect. Other provisions, however, such as the establishment of ethics committees on the use of animals, have been effective in ensuring that lab animals receive humane treatment. However, animal rights activists still believe that much abuse continues to go undetected.

Many research labs have adopted reforms on their

own. For example, New York University's Laboratory for Experimental Medicine and Surgery in Primates (LEMSIP) makes a special effort to keep the 250 chimpanzees used in AIDS and hepatitis research mentally and emotionally stimulated. Veterinarian James Mahoney has built wire-mesh tunnels connecting the chimps' cages to encourage social contact. Plexiglas windows allow the chimps to see each other even if they must be kept separate for an experiment. To keep the chimpanzees from becoming bored, Mahoney gives them long pieces of plastic tubing and puts tubs of frozen Kool-Aid outside their cages. The chimps spend hours getting drinks of Kool-Aid by using the plastic tubing like straws.

Where research animals come from

Laboratories get their research animals from several sources. Research facilities may breed their own animals or purchase them from companies that specialize in raising laboratory animals. Monkeys and chimpanzees are sometimes imported from foreign countries where they are captured in the wild. In some states animal shelters are required by law to provide dogs and cats for research. This process is called pound seizure.

A pound seizure law requires state-supported animal shelters to turn excess animals over to research facilities. Today, five states—Iowa, Minnesota, South Dakota, Utah, and Oklahoma—and the District of Columbia have pound seizure laws. About 2 percent of the more than fifteen million unwanted dogs and cats left in pounds and shelters each year are used in research. Most of the rest of these animals are destroyed because new homes cannot be found for them.

Even though the number of pets that eventually find their way to research labs is relatively small, animal welfare and animal rights groups are united in opposing pound seizure. Nancy Payton, an offi-

Some animals used in medical research come from animal shelters, as did this dog. Researchers later implanted a plastic heart valve in the dog.

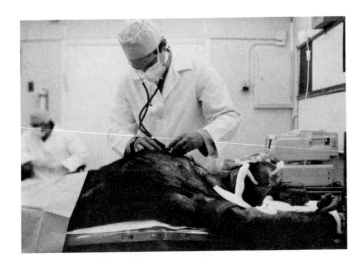

Many research facilities that use animals argue that they plan operations with the same care and use the same high quality facilities as they would for human patients.

cer of the Massachusetts Society for the Protection of Animals testified against pound seizure before the Massachusetts legislature. In her testimony, she said, "a) Unclaimed animals (many of which are former pets) are the least suitable candidates for research from a humane viewpoint because the research laboratory atmosphere is foreign and threatening; b) responsible animal control is undermined by pound seizure laws because many people, believing that animals brought to a public pound may be surrendered for research, will abandon them instead; and c) pound seizure encourages the view that laboratory animals are cheap, disposable tools."

According to *In Defense of Animals,* edited by Peter Singer, twelve states currently ban or limit the use of pound animals in biomedical research: Connecticut, Delaware, Hawaii, Maine, Maryland, Masachusetts, New Hampshire, New Jersey, New York, Pennsylvania, Vermont, and Rhode Island. In other states pound seizure is regulated by county or city laws.

Although supporters of animal research usually talk about the medical advances made possible by animal experimentation, less than half of the lab animals in this country are used for medical research.

INTRODUCING THE ALTERNATIVE.

Some cosmetics manufacturers test their products on animals. The cosmetics company Beauty Without Cruelty does not, and points this out in its advertisements.

Most are used by manufacturers of cosmetics and household products in toxicity testing. Toxicity testing measures how poisonous a substance is. Almost every new product, from car wax to eye shadow, is tested on animals before it is sold to the public.

Draize Eye Irritancy and LD50 tests

Toxicity tests performed on animals, like the Draize Eye Irritancy Test and the LD50, are used to determine the safety of today's consumer products. But there is a negative side to the Draize and LD50 tests. Because anesthesia would interfere with the test results, it cannot be given to the test animals, and the procedures are therefore very painful for them.

The Draize Eye Irritancy Test is designed to measure the harm a product might do if accidentally spilled into someone's eye. Because a rabbit's eye does not produce many tears that might wash away the irritant, the test is usually performed on albino rabbits. Many of the 500,000 rabbits used annually in research facilities undergo the Draize test. The test is performed by placing between six and nine albino rabbits in a device that holds them still. Then technicians drop a small amount of the product into one eye of each rabbit. The other eye is used for comparison purposes. They use a scoring system to describe the condition of the treated eye, which can range from mildly irritated to completely destroyed. The product must score within a certain range to be considered safe by federal agencies. The rabbits are euthanatized at the end of the test so that they will not continue to suffer.

The LD50 test, which stands for "lethal dose 50 percent," tells researchers how much of a drug or product is needed to kill half the animals exposed to it. It was developed during the 1920s when the strength of important but powerful drugs like insulin and diphtheria antitoxin varied from batch to batch. The LD50 was used as a standard to measure the correct dosage for humans. Today, sophisticated chemical tests evaluate the strength of most drugs, but the LD50 continues to be used to measure how poisonous household products are.

The test is performed by feeding or injecting rats, mice, or other small animals different amounts of test material. Many of the test animals die, and all

Bloom County by Berke Breathed © 1989 Washington Post Writers Group. Reprinted with permission.

become very sick. Researchers record the number of animals that die within a set length of time. That number is converted to an LD50 value. Manufacturers use the LD50 value as a measure of their products' safety.

These two tests are highly controversial because all the animals used suffer a great deal of pain. Are the Draize test and LD50 really necessary? There is much evidence that proves these tests are not. The Draize test, for example, has been criticized for being inaccurate. For one thing, the sensitivity of a rabbit's eye to the test material is far greater than a human's would be. A 1979 survey of twenty-four laboratories found that the Draize test is also unreliable. For example, cream peroxide passed the test in some laboratories and failed it in others. Dr. Frederick Sperling, a well-known toxicologist, concluded that he did not support the test, "which is not a good one scientifically. . . . It is deplorable that better testing for primary skin and eye irritation has not been developed in the approximately 40 years of its use."

Dangerous tests

Other toxicologists are even more critical of the LD50 test. S.B. Baker says that such tests "are of little use and are expensive in animals. The main information they give is an indication of the size of dose required to commit suicide." LD50 results also vary

Rabbits have been used to test eye irritancy levels of cosmetics and other products. The National Anti-Vivisection Society notes its opposition to such practices in this advertisement.

Demonstrators protest the use of Draize tests on rabbits in New Jersey. These people contend that manufacturers can find other means of testing the safety of their products.

greatly, even between related species. In one test, one chemical was given to both male albino rats and male albino mice. The amount needed to kill the mice was much higher than the amount needed to kill the rats. With such a difference between similar species, the value of applying those results to humans is unclear.

U.S. law requires that all products be proven safe for the public, but it does not specify the use of animals in testing. Yet manufacturers continue to use the Draize test and LD50.

There are three reasons for the continuing use of these tests. First, the Draize test and LD50 have been used for so long (forty years) that they have become industry standards. Second, international standards require the Draize test or LD50, so that any manufacturer who wishes to sell a product overseas must use one of these tests anyway. Finally, insurance companies and corporate lawyers often insist that manufacturers conduct the tests to prove the safety of their products.

Alternatives to animal testing

Animal advocates such as the American Fund for Alternatives to Animal Research and several other organizations are working with scientists to develop alternatives to animal testing.

They call their plan the three *R*s of animal experimentation: replacement, reduction, and refinement. Total replacement of animals with nonanimal alternatives is the eventual goal. Still, some types of experiments will need animal subjects until replacements can be developed. In the meantime, the American Fund for Alternatives to Animal Research teaches experimenters how to reduce number of animals used. Where animals must be used, developers try to refine current procedures to avoid unnecessary pain or stress to the animals.

A number of alternative methods have been developed. Many of them are less expensive and more accurate than animal testing. One method uses computers to substitute for the LD50 test. Another method uses cultures of single-celled organisms. The cells and various concentrations of the test chemical are placed together, along with a special red dye. Only living cells take up the dye, so cultures of healthy cells turn pink, while cultures in which the cells have died remain pale. Yet another method replaces living rabbit eyes in the Draize test with human eyes from eye banks or with the tissue that lines chicken eggs. Manufacturers can also avoid testing altogether by using previously tested ingredients, natural ingredients, or warning labels.

A recent poll conducted by *Advertising Age* mag-

azine and the Gallup Organization found that 60 percent of consumers say they oppose animal testing on cosmetics. In response to public demand, a number of cosmetic firms—including Avon, Revlon, Pond's, and Faberge—have abandoned animal testing. Mary Kay Cosmetics and Amway Corporation have declared moratoriums on animal testing, and the Noxell Corporation has decided to replace the Draize test with laboratory tests that do not require animals. These companies are responding to the change in public attitudes prompted by many animal rights organizations.

There have been other successful efforts to minimize the use of animals while conducting needed research. The National Anti-Vivisection Society, for example, sponsors classes in alternatives to animal testing for scientists. Some universities include ethics classes that stress the humane, responsible treatment of research animals. And animal advocates have been included on the institutional care and use committees that review plans for animal research.

Other ways to help reduce animal experimentation have yet to be tried. Research facilities, scientific organizations, and universities could make it clear that they expect their researchers to show consideration and sensitivity toward their animal subjects. The federal government could publish a list of approved tests that do not use animals and encourage foreign agencies to accept them in place of the Draize test and LD50. Finally, researchers themselves could at least consider the idea that ending the use of animals sometime in the future is a worthwhile goal.

3

Animals in Education

W HEN FELLOW STUDENTS saw Jenifer Graham walking through the halls of her Southern California high school, they would crouch down and croak like frogs, "Ribbit, ribbit!" Everyone knew who Jenifer was. She was the "frog girl."

Jenifer's troubles began in 1986 when she refused to dissect a frog in her biology class. Jenifer, a good student with a deep belief against killing animals, offered to do the work using models or computers. School officials said she was "just making trouble." They insisted that Jenifer transfer to another class, dissect the frog, or get a low grade and a note on her transcript that she had not participated. But Jenifer needed the class to go to college. She stayed in the class, but she did not dissect the frog.

With legal assistance from the American Humane Society of the United States, Jenifer sued the school. She said her right to freedom of religion had been violated. Jenifer won. The school had to provide an alternative way for her to earn a grade.

(opposite page) These mice are part of an experiment on the effects of sound conducted at the University of California at Davis. Medical and veterinary schools use about fifty thousand animals annually for surgery and instruction on anatomy.

Many people were interested in Jenifer's case. The California legislature agreed that Jenifer had a right to say "no." In 1987 it passed a law that requires schools to provide alternative assignments for students who refuse to dissect animals because of their

53

Jenifer Graham (left) went to court rather than dissect a frog in her high school biology class. The California Legislature later passed a law requiring schools to provide alternative assignments for students who refuse to dissect animals because of their beliefs.

beliefs. In 1989, CBS television broadcast her story as an "After School Special." So many people called Jenifer that she and her mother got help from the Animal Legal Defense Fund (ALDF) to set up a national toll-free hot line. The hot line answers questions and counsels students who are upset about doing dissections.

"It's not right to kill animals," Jenifer says, "especially for unnecessary reasons like dissection. It would be different if I were going to veterinary school. After all, I wouldn't want to take my dog to a vet who doesn't know anything about its insides. But in high school I can learn some, if not more, by using alternative methods."

Animals in many classrooms

Every year, more than five million frogs are dissected in U.S. junior and senior high schools. Other animals—dogs, cats, pigs, rabbits, and mice—are also killed and dissected. In U.S. medical and veterinary schools, about fifty thousand animals, most of them dogs, are used yearly to give students practice in surgery and to demonstrate physiological principles.

What do students learn from so many animals in the classroom? Rosalina Hairston of the National Association of Biology Teachers (NABT) says that animals are used for a variety of purposes, depending on the ages and maturity of the students.

In elementary school, teachers keep animals in the classroom for two reasons. Teachers use them to teach children about responsible pet ownership, and class pets help children explore the relationship between humans and animals. Young students are en-

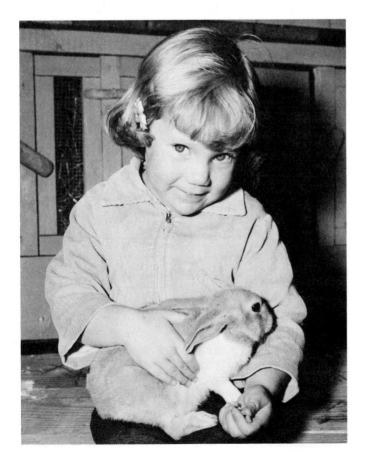

Young children like this girl often learn about the relationship between humans and animals in their elementary school classrooms.

couraged to hold or stroke cuddly animals. This experience helps them talk or write about animals.

In junior high school or middle school, animals are usually found only in science classrooms. Students study specific animals, usually frogs, fish, and earthworms, to learn how animals relate to their environment. They learn about animal physiology —how animals breathe, eat, excrete, and reproduce. Some classes require students to dissect dead earthworms or frogs. From these activities students learn about the processes of life and acquire observation skills.

In high school biology, students learn experimental procedures by dissecting frogs and other animals. Students are expected to behave like young scientists. They hypothesize, or make an educated guess,

about what the results of an experiment will be, then record the actual results.

In college, physiology and anatomy students dissect cats, dogs, frogs, and other animals to learn the parts of the body and discover how they interact. Other students use animals in psychology experiments. Finally, medical and veterinary students practice surgery and other medical techniques on animals.

The value of animals in the classroom

Educators value the experiences students have with animals in the classroom. The National Science Teachers Association (NSTA) states, "Study of living organisms is essential for an understanding of living processes."

Many teachers believe in the educational worth of dissection. George Zahrobsky, a former president of the National Association of Biology Teachers, says, "Dissection is the rediscovery of how life works. It teaches us how organisms operate in a wonderfully complex world." The NABT policy statement on the use of animals in biology reinforces Zahrobsky's statement: "The dissection of animals has a long and well established place in the teaching of life sciences. . . . Dissection activities conducted by thoughtful instructors can illustrate important and enduring principles in biology."

The California State Department of Education believes dissection is educationally important, but it also accepts a student's right to refuse to dissect. The Department says, "Dissection offers unique insights and a profound appreciation of the relationship between internal structures and their functions. Dissections enable students to gain fine lab motor skills [skills in using their hands] and attendant safety procedures. These skills and acquired knowledge empower students with increased self-confidence for continued success in future science courses."

Although many educators approve of the varied

These Soviet medical students learn more about how the body functions by discussing and viewing a dog with transplanted heart and lungs.

uses of animals in the classroom, animal advocates do not. It is their belief that the routine use of animals as teaching tools harms students as well as animals. The ASPCA says that students do not need hands-on experience to learn about science. Animal experimentation in schools is not designed to gather new information. Instead, most educational projects give students practice in various techniques or demonstrate effects that are already well known. The Humane Society claims that many students are so upset

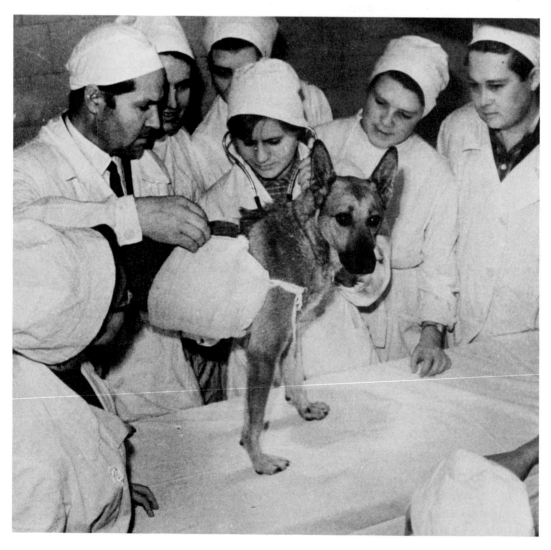

by dissecting or experimenting on animals that they avoid taking science classes.

Andrew Rowan, although a trained scientist himself, believes that high school biology classes often teach students to see the animal as an object. This approach to life science encourages students to distance themselves from the animals they study and to shut off emotions or sensibilities that interfere with the collection of information. Rowan says students learn that anything they do to an experimental animal is "scientific" and that any ethical concerns they might have about the animal are sentimental and "unscientific." Rowan concludes that this approach may cause students to fail to develop the skills of self-criticism and intuition necessary for top-quality research. They may ignore signs in animals that show the experiment is not working. One of the areas Rowan and others see this lack of sensitivity is in school science fairs.

Science fairs

School science fairs have received a great deal of criticism for allowing students to use animals in individual science projects. The idea for science fairs originated in 1942, when Westinghouse began sponsoring the Science Talent Search. The purpose of the talent search was to discover talented students and encourage them to become scientists. The search has been successful. To date, four past national winners of the competition have gone on to win the Nobel Prize. In 1950, a second national science competition, the International Science and Engineering Fair (ISEF), began. Originally, both competitions encouraged entries involving animal experimentation.

In 1969, there were many experiments that used animals in the Westinghouse Science Talent Search. One award winner performed skin grafts on one thousand mice. Another winner performed brain

This high school student X-rayed mice to study the effects of radiation for a 1950s science fair. Science fair experiments that cause pain or suffering in animals were later banned.

surgery on twenty-five mice. (Most of the mice died.) The $250 prize went to an experiment that involved removing the eyeballs of five house sparrows. The experiment was supposed to discover whether the birds could avoid electric shocks and find food at the end of a box. Instead, the birds starved to death.

A *New York Times* editorial condemned the experiments, calling them "atrocious." "Science fairs at the local, state and national level often award prizes to students whose only real achievement has been the deliberate or inadvertent [accidental] torture of animals," the editorial said. In response to the public uproar, Westinghouse revised its rules to forbid experiments that caused pain or suffering to animals.

But ISEF continued to accept projects involving animal experiments until 1980. At that time, the National Science Teachers Association set standards that specifically forbid the use of vertebrate animals, or animals with backbones that have nervous systems capable of feeling pain, in experiments that would cause pain or discomfort to the animals. As recently as 1982, the ISEF in Houston featured animal experiments that violated the NSTA rules. One project displayed photographs of animals that had been fed only cookies, french fries, chewing gum, and lollipops. Another involved forcing a pregnant rat to drink a toxic solution to learn what the effect on her offspring would be.

Science teachers respond that many of these experiments have been banned. Few science fairs still accept animal experiments. And a number of states, such as California, have laws banning students from experimenting on living animals.

Alternatives to animal experiments

The National Science Teachers Association and the National Association of Biology Teachers have responded to the growing criticism of dissection and vivisection by issuing guidelines for the use of animals in the classroom. Their recommendations follow the three *R*s of reduction, refinement, and replacement.

The NSTA Code of Practice on Animals in Schools stresses that "this study [of animals]. . .must go hand-in-hand with observations of humane principles of animal care and treatment." It limits experimental procedures performed on vertebrate animals to "those that do not involve pain or discomfort to the animal." It recommends using plants, bacteria, worms, snails, or other invertebrate animals, animals

"Sure it looks easy! But if you get to the cheese, they try to give you cancer!"

without backbones, in experiments with living organisms. Animals without backbones have less developed nervous systems and are thought to feel little or no pain. The code also bans behavioral experiments that punish animals with shocks. Experimenters are told to use rewards instead, such as teaching a rat to run a maze by placing food at the end of the maze.

The NABT policy statement on "The Responsible Use of Animals in Biology Classrooms," admits that "it is timely to reexamine the use of animals in precollege education." The policy statement continues, "The National Association of Biology Teachers believes that all biology teachers should foster a respect for life and should teach about the interrelationship and interdependency of all living things. Furthermore, they should teach that humans must care for the fragile web of life that exists on this planet. In light of this principle, NABT supports alternatives to dissection and vivisection wherever possible in the biology curricula."

NABT does not favor removing animals from the classroom. Instead, it recommends observing animal behavior and learning how to take care of animals. Other alternatives include increased experimentation with plants and invertebrate animals, the use of computer simulations, videotaped demonstrations, and increased emphasis on the organism as it relates to its environment.

Does the student have a choice?

A number of students, including Jenifer Graham, have tried to establish their right to refuse to participate in experimentation. The outcome of these cases has been mixed. When the student's refusal is the result of a moral or spiritual belief, however, legal authorities say that in many cases the student's position will be protected by the First Amendment or similar state laws.

The Animal Legal Defense Fund has prepared the following list of suggestions for students who do not wish to participate in vivisection or dissection:

1. Know yourself and how far you are prepared to go in order to establish your right not to vivisect/dissect.

2. Before the term starts, or as soon as possible, ask whether you will be required to dissect or use live animals. Do not presume that the use of animals will be mentioned in the course outline.

Bloom County by Berke Brethed © 1988 Washington Post Writers Group. Reprinted with permission.

3. Raise your objections at the earliest possible time. Do not wait until the day of the dissection class or until the term is almost completed to voice your objections.

4. Approach your teacher either alone or with like-minded classmates. State your objection and be prepared to discuss the reasons for your refusal to vivisect or dissect.

5. Never approach the teacher in an arrogant, self-righteous, or confrontational manner. Presume that he or she has a different belief system on the issue of animal use. It is unlikely that you will change his or her views.

6. Present a reasonable alternative project that will teach you the planned lesson by some method that does not use animals. This could include a book report, graphs or diagrams of the animal's organs, an interview with an expert on the subject, or some other project. The project should take an equal amount of time and effort. It should not be a punishment for your failure to attend the vivisection or dissection laboratory.

7. Ask your teacher to reply to your request promptly, so you will have enough time to complete the alternative project.

8. Expect resistance to your objections. Be prepared to discuss your beliefs and principles in a non-judgmental way. Your refusal may be threatening to your teacher. Be both firm and polite.

9. At all times, document your actions by keeping a written record of dates, times, people involved, and the substance of all conversations. If you send written notes to your teacher or administrative personnel, keep copies for your files.

10. If you need legal advice or help, contact the Animal Legal Defense Fund. The ALDF will help you negotiate with your school administrators.

Many educators are responding to the increasing public concern for animal welfare and are taking a second look at the role of animals in the classroom today. While most schools encourage scientific investigation using animals, there are now alternatives for students with strong personal beliefs against dissection. New standards adopted by the NABT and other associations encourage the humane use of animals. This new sensitivity may make the study of science more appealing to the average person.

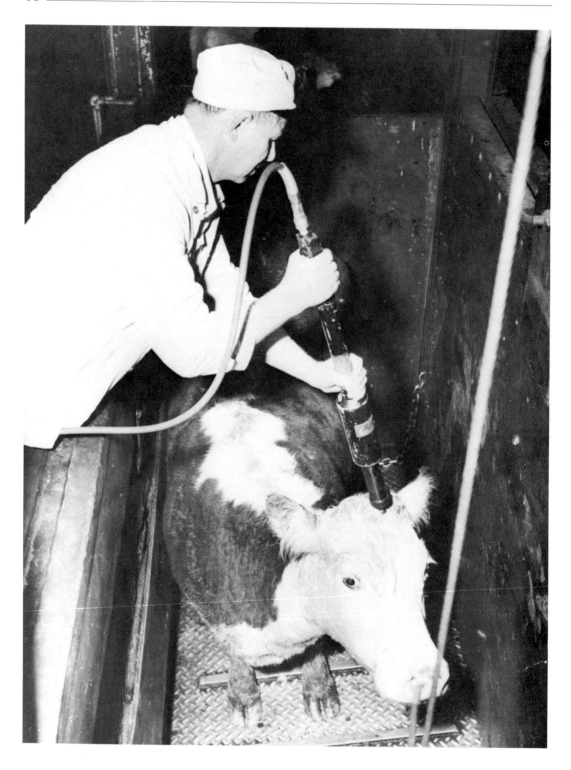

4

Animal Industries

THE STORYBOOK FARM—a red barn, a yard full of chickens, a few pigs wallowing in the mud, and a dozen milk cows in the pasture—has almost disappeared in the past fifty years. All over the world, methods of raising farm animals have changed. The traditional small-scale farm has been replaced by automated "confinement facilities" —huge, warehouse-like barns where animals are kept indoors for most of their lives. On the positive side, these large operations allow modern farmer-businesspeople to produce meat, milk, and eggs in a shorter time and at a lower cost. But the negative side is the way farm animals are treated to produce these results.

This new approach to farming is known as agribusiness. It is the result of private and government research costing billions of dollars. Farmers' organizations like the Animal Industry Foundation (AIF) praise the "improved animal housing, handling practices, and healthy, nutritious feeds" that allow 3 percent of the U.S. population to produce more than enough food for everyone in the country at reasonable prices.

Animal rights groups, however, condemn agribusiness, calling it "factory farming." They say new farming techniques are designed only to gain the most profit with the least amount of effort. Activists

(opposite page) A slaughterhouse worker demonstrates what is considered a humane method of killing animals before a slaughter. Here, he uses an air-powered stun gun that produces instantaneous unconsciousness in the animal.

67

Typically, three to five egg-laying hens are squeezed into a single wire battery cage, leaving each bird an area smaller than a piece of typing paper.

accuse factory farmers of having no concern for the physical or social well-being of their animals. Because of publicity generated by animal rights groups, the methods used by farmers have been examined more closely. Not only have these methods been attacked because people believe they are inhumane, but some practices, like adding medicines to animals' feed, are questioned as being dangerous to human health.

The problem is complicated by the fact that farm animals are not covered by the Animal Welfare Act, the only federal animal protection law. As Bradley Miller, executive director of the Humane Farming Association, says, "There is *no* inspection of farms in our country to ensure humane treatment of animals. While local animal welfare laws do cover farm animals, they are designed to protect them from individual malicious acts, like beating a calf. But there's another standard for common practices on the farm. Humane treatment is left up to the individual producer." These different opinions over how animals should be treated is at the heart of the debate over factory farming. Several common farming practices are criticized by the animal rights groups.

Chickens

On these new farms, hens are raised to be either those who will lay eggs, or broilers, those who will be sold for their meat. More than 90 percent of all chickens are hatched and produced under the following conditions.

The chickens raised to produce eggs live about one year in "battery cages." The floor space in these small, wire pens measures approximately twelve inches long by eighteen inches wide. A single battery cage holds between three and five birds, allowing each 4.5-pound bird between forty-three and seventy-two square inches of living space—an area smaller than a piece of typing paper.

Between 50,000 and 100,000 laying chickens are kept in the average henhouse. Their battery cages are stacked three or four levels high. The small cages give the chickens little room to stretch their wings or groom their feathers. The sloping wire cage floor, designed to make egg collection easier, prevents the birds from perching.

Everything is automated. Conveyer belts carry away the eggs, machines deliver feed and water, and even waste is scraped from beneath the birds' cages by a machine.

Under these cramped conditions, hens often in-

Battery cages leave little room for chickens to stretch their wings or groom their feathers. The sloping floors make egg collection easier but prevent the birds from perching.

jure themselves. Without space to clean their own injuries and without care from their human keepers, these injuries often develop into sores. Other birds peck at the injuries. Cannibalism, or eating other animals of the same species, is common among these hens. To prevent aggressive behavior, the amount of light in the henhouse is kept low and the birds' upper beak is cut off with a hot blade.

Almost all laying chickens are of the white leghorn variety. Members of this breed are capable of producing 250 eggs a year. When the layers are about eighteen months old, they begin to produce fewer eggs of poorer quality. Then the hens are sold as stewing chickens or pet food, or they are forced to molt.

Molting, or the shedding of feathers, is a natural process in all birds. In nature, birds shed their feathers and become inactive in the darkest and coldest part of winter. Female birds do not lay eggs until

Chickens raised for meat typically live in huge sheds. Dim lights remain on all the time to stimulate feeding. Here, a Missouri poultry farmer removes chickens killed by extremely hot weather.

their new feathers have grown in. Molting allows the birds' bodies to rest before beginning another breeding cycle.

Under factory farm conditions, where the light and temperature are constant, chickens will not molt unless dramatic changes are made in their environment. To induce a molt, the lights are turned off and food and water are withheld from the laying hens for up to four days. Then the birds are given water and a small amount of low-protein feed. These conditions cause the birds to shed their feathers. Some birds die, and the Humane Farming Association estimates that between 5 and 25 percent of the flock does not survive a forced molt. The entire molt cycle takes from six to eight weeks. When it is completed, the surviving hens have grown new feathers and are capable of producing high-quality eggs once more.

Broilers, chickens raised for their meat, spend their short lives (about seven to eight weeks) on the floors of huge sheds. A single flock usually contains ten thousand to seventy thousand birds of both sexes. The dim lights stay on twenty-four hours a day to stimulate feeding. Because it has been proven that low doses of antibiotics cause weight gain, the birds routinely receive antibiotics in their water.

When it is time for the broilers to go to the slaughterhouse, poultry workers wade through the thousands of birds, catching them and putting them onto trucks. More than four billion chickens are raised and slaughtered in this fashion each year.

Hogs

The average American eats seventy pounds of pork and pork products annually. According to the Animal Protection Institute of America, of the ninety-four million hogs born in the United States every year, about 90 percent spend part of their lives in confinement.

Piglets are born in a farrowing crate, a narrow stall designed to keep the sow, or mother pig, from crushing or even eating one of her piglets. The crate allows her little freedom of movement. She cannot turn around or move more than a step or two in any direction.

The young pigs are taken away from their mother as soon as possible so that she can be rebred. After she is impregnated again, the sow may be kept in a gestation crate, another narrow pen with metal or concrete flooring. Sometimes, she is chained to the front of the pen. An estimated two million sows are kept in gestation crates each year.

Once separated from their mother, the piglets are put in small pens stacked two or three tiers high. Their tails are clipped to prevent tail biting, which young pigs do as a result of boredom and over-crowding.

An inspector watches as hogs are removed for slaughter. Typically, hogs are slaughtered once they reach 210 to 220 pounds.

After they reach a weight of 50 pounds, the piglets are moved to "finishing pens." There, they are fed corn and are fattened for slaughter. The pens allow the pigs as little as six square feet of floor space apiece. The animals grow rapidly, reaching a market weight of 210 to 220 pounds in about four months.

Cattle

Two kinds of cattle are used in modern farming operations: dairy cattle and beef cattle. Dairy cows are often kept in herds out of doors then brought into specially equipped barns to be milked. Herds kept indoors sometimes live in barns with stanchions, devices that fit around the cows' necks and tie them to their stalls. The milking machines are brought in to them. Or the cows live in free-stall barns, where they move from their stalls to a milking parlor or feed troughs.

Due to selective breeding, an American dairy cow today produces 2.5 times as much milk as her ancestors did thirty years ago. Farmers now expect to get between twelve thousand and sixteen thousand pounds of milk per year from each cow. Cows give milk for about ten months after the birth of each calf. To make sure cows continue to produce milk, farmers rebreed them soon after each calf is born.

Calves are separated from their mothers at about three to four days of age. Male calves and poor-quality female calves are sold to veal operations. Veal is the meat from calves.

The raising of white, or milk-fed, veal is an expanding industry in the United States. Each year, between 750,000 and 1 million calves are raised in crates or other small, enclosed areas and fed a "milk replacer" low in iron that will produce pale-colored meat. Gourmets consider this type of veal superior to that produced from grass-fed calves or calves that

With selective breeding, American dairy cows today produce more than twice as much milk as dairy cows produced thirty years ago.

Dairy cows often live outdoors until they are brought into specially equipped barns for milking.

were slaughtered when they were only two or three days old. Top-quality veal can bring the farmer as much as fourteen dollars a pound.

Veal calves live restricted lives. They are not allowed to run about or eat grass or hay because it might affect the color, tenderness, and texture of their flesh. Because veal calves become ill easily, they are usually fed antibiotics in their food and kept separate from one another. They live in individual stalls, some of them small crates that measure just two feet wide and five feet long. When the veal calves reach 350 pounds at about sixteen weeks of age, they are slaughtered. By then, the calves in the small crates have no room to move around or even to lie down.

Beef cattle do not experience such restrictions and are seldom raised in confinement. These remain with their mothers on the range until they are weaned, or made to take food other than by nursing, at about seven months of age. After weaning, the male calves and unwanted female calves are either sold or shipped to feedlots, where they are fattened for market.

Before shipment, the male calves are castrated, or have their testicles removed. Their horns may also

Veal calves often are kept in small, individual stalls like those pictured here. The stalls prevent the calves from moving or lying down.

After 120 to 150 days in feedlots, most steer are large enough for slaughter.

be cut off. The calves are castrated to prevent their bodies from naturally producing testosterone. Testosterone is undesirable in beef cattle because it causes them to be aggressive and toughens their meat. The castrated calves will be less aggressive than normal. Cattle ranchers remove the animals' horns so that they will not injure one another during shipping.

In the feedlot, the castrated calves, now known as steers, are fed a concentrated diet rich in grain, which produces the desired amount of fat in their meat. The rich food often gives the steers digestive problems, so they are fed antibiotics as well as hormones to make them put on weight faster. After 120 to 150 days in the feedlot, the steers are large enough for slaughter.

Four to five billion farm animals are raised annually in the United States. A few animal rights groups, such as the Farm Animal Reform Movement and the Humane Farming Association, dedicate themselves to changing the treatment of farm animals. As Bradley Miller claims, "We want to reform current practices. Is it humane to keep a veal calf in a crate so small that it can't turn around?"

Activists who work to reform farming have goals similar to those of the people who fight animal rights battles on other fronts. They want animals to be able to live more natural lives. They want chickens to be able to walk around and hunt and scratch for food in sand, cows and calves to be able to live together, pigs to be able to raise their piglets in large pens where they can exhibit their natural behavior. While farmers counter that these practices are inefficient, animal activists believe they are necessary for treating animals humanely. Miller criticizes the farm industry as being too concerned with profits and says, "They treat animals more or less like crops as if animals did not need to walk. Millions of farm animals are forced to live in crates barely larger than their bodies, where they cannot stretch their limbs or move around. If we were to do this to a dog or cat—or even an animal in a laboratory—we could be arrested."

Organizations that support these current farming practices, such as the Animal Industry Foundation, respond that American methods of raising livestock do not harm animals. The AIF claims, "Farmers and ranchers are neither cruel nor naive. . . . One of the main reasons someone goes into farming or ranching

By permission of Johnny Hart and NAS, Inc.

is a desire to work with animals." Farmers argue that they enjoy farming and animals but that they are realistic about why they farm. They treat farm animals, which are raised to be killed, differently from domestic family pets. Farmers resent being called cruel and believe animal rights activists are sentimental and overly emotional about farm practices.

In addition, farmers argue that they have a financial stake in treating their animals well. No meat packaging plant will buy a pig, cow, or chicken that is underfed or unhealthy. As the AIF argues, "A farmer would compromise his or her own welfare if animals were mistreated. Agriculture is very competitive in the U.S., a career which pays the farmer a slim profit on the animals he cares for. It is in the farmer's own best interest to see the animals in his charge are treated humanely, guaranteeing him a healthy, high-quality animal, a greater return on his investment, and a wholesome food product." Although profit does motivate farmers, as animal rights activists claim, farmers say that the profit motive ensures animals are kept healthy.

Is factory farm food safe?

Animal rights advocates often raise the question of food safety in their fight to reform farm practices. They claim that meat, milk, and eggs produced in factory farms are contaminated with antibiotics and hormones. "We are all so full of antibiotics now that they're coming out our ears," Astrid Lindgren, a Swedish animal advocate, says.

In fact, according to the Center for Science in the Public Interest, half of the antibiotics produced in the United States each year are used on farm animals. Dr. Marc Lappe, professor of public health at the University of California at Berkeley, reports that 90 percent of the country's swine and veal calves are fed antibiotics. About 75 percent of all cattle, 50 percent of sheep, and virtually all poultry routinely receive antibiotics.

Artificial hormones are regularly added to the feed eaten by cattle. Synthetic hormones, such as zeranol and trenbolene, make beef cattle grow faster and quicker.

The side effects of feed additives

Is the use of antibiotics and hormones in food animals harmful to humans? The U.S. Food and Drug Administration (USDA), which sets the levels of allowable hormone and antibiotic use in food, says that the doses are safe for human consumption. The USDA Food and Safety Inspection Service inspects milk, meat, and eggs to insure that products with high residues of drugs or hormones do not reach consumers.

Evidence does exist, however, that the wide-spread practice of adding antibiotics to animal feed is producing strains of "superbugs," bacteria that are resistant to standard antibiotics. Dr. Scott Holmberg of the Federal Centers for Disease Control documented an attack of one superbug, a resistant strain of salmonella. Salmonella, which kills approximately 550 people in the U.S. annually, causes violent stomach upset in humans.

Holmberg traced an outbreak of salmonella poisoning in eighteen people to hamburgers made from cattle who had been fed the antibiotic tetracycline on one farm in North Dakota. He found that twelve of the eighteen sick people were already taking antibiotics when they came down with the disease. Holmberg concluded that the antibiotics were ineffective against the superstrain of salmonella.

While livestock industry is aware of this problem, it believes the use of these additives is not harmful. "Animal drugs include antibiotics to prevent and treat animal disease," the AIF says. "There are also antibiotics used in humans that are also used in animals. There is now an unresolved scientific debate

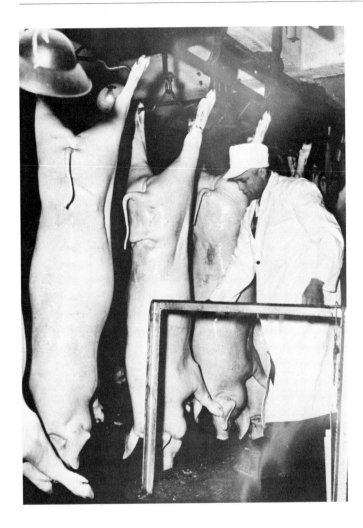

These slaughtered pigs probably received large doses of antibiotics. This practice calls into question the healthiness of pork, chicken, and beef.

over these uses. Since there is no conclusive scientific proof that the use of human antibiotics in animals—a practice going back thirty-five years—is a risk to human health, these products are used to prevent and treat illness in some animals, in addition to aiding growth." While farmers and animal activists are often at opposite ends in their attitudes, some people are working toward alternative solutions for farming practices.

In Sweden, Astrid Lindgren, creator of the character Pippi Longstocking, wrote a series of articles about factory farm practices she considers inhumane. The series resulted in an animal protection law that activists consider a model for other countries.

Sweden's New Animal Protection Law, passed in 1988, forbids many factory farm practices, such as chaining sows to their pens. Cattle, pigs, and chickens must be allowed freedom of movement. Farmers must provide their animals clean bedding and separate feeding and sleeping places. No drugs or hormones can be used on farm animals except to treat disease, and all slaughter is to be "as humane as possible." Will this sort of law ever pass in the United States?

Probably not, say animal rights advocates like the Humane Farming Association's Bradley Miller. In 1989, a referendum on animal rights was put on the ballot in Massachusetts. It was defeated, with 73 percent of the electorate voting against it. Bradley Miller and others conclude that reforms will come gradually, one at a time. Among the changes that

How's it prepared? First we chop off its head; then we rip its feathers off, then . . .

From the Spring 1988 *Conscience*, published by Canadian Vegans for Animal Rights.

have been suggested, the following seem the most likely.

Methods of raising veal calves will change. Ferdinand Metz, head of the Culinary Institute of America, has publicly announced that "pink veal tastes exactly the same [as white veal]. There is no difference." And even Dan Murphy, editor of *Meat Processing* magazine, has come out in favor of ending the crate system. "Fact is, it won't be the end of the world if the public can't dine on so-called 'white' veal," he told his readers in a 1989 editorial. Farm experts are already working to perfect a system where veal calves can be raised in groups.

Other reforms are already underway. Some ranchers in the Southwest sell beef that has not been fattened in feedlots. Health food stores carry eggs from chickens that have not been confined in battery cages. Farm cooperatives and other suppliers produce poultry and pork that have been range-fed, or allowed to move around freely.

5

Other Animal Industries

OTHER ANIMAL INDUSTRIES conducted on farms, such as fur ranching and raising puppies for sale to pet shops, are also being debated. In the case of the fur controversy, animal rights groups question both the methods used in raising fur-bearing animals and the morality of wearing coats made from these animals.

Twenty-three percent of all furs produced in the United States are from animals raised on fur ranches, a total of 5.6 million animals in 1986. Ranch-raised animals include mink, rabbit, and chinchilla. These animals are kept in small cages, sometimes hardly bigger than the animal itself. These small cages make the animals nervous, and they often constantly pace back and forth or chew and lick themselves until they develop open sores.

When the animals are large enough, ranchers kill them in ways that will not harm their pelts—by electrocution, neck breaking, poison, or exposure to chloroform or car exhaust. Large animals like foxes are usually electrocuted, and small animals like weasels and minks often have their necks broken. Animal rights activists object to such practices, saying the animals experience too much pain before they die. Electrocution, for example, sometimes

(opposite page) Members of an animal rights organization called Trans-Species Unlimited carry a casket filled with furs in protest of the killing of animals for coats. They believe synthetic products have made the use of animal fur unnecessary.

Television personality Bob Barker leads an antifur demonstration in New York City. Marchers urged New Yorkers not to buy fur coats.

must be repeated a couple of times before the animal is finally dead.

Ranchers who raise animals for furs, however, do not feel remorse about their methods. They see themselves as providing a product that people want and they believe they use reasonable methods to produce the furs. Inhumane treatment is impossible, ranchers claim, for it would hurt the animals' coats. "The better the care [fur ranchers] provide, the better the fur product," Robert Buckler of the Fur Farms Animals Welfare Coalition explains.

Is wearing a fur immoral?

Most animal rights activists object to all fur ranching. Quality synthetic products, such as polyester fill, have made furs obsolete, these people argue. As Trans-Species Unlimited, an animal rights organization explains, "There is absolutely no excuse for killing animals to produce unnecessary luxury garments. Plenty of alternative garments are readily available, which are of equal or superior quality, cost less, require less energy to produce, are just as warm, and involve no animal suffering." A Fund for Animals ad reads, "Raccoon Coat: Price $7,000 and 40 Raccoons."

Celebrities like Rue McClanahan and Loretta Switt have appeared in commercials urging the public not to buy furs, and clothing designer Bill Blass has announced that he will stop designing furs. Bob Barker resigned as host of the Miss USA and Miss Universe pageants when officials announced that they would be awarding the winners fur coats. "It isn't necessary to torture and kill animals to show how much money you have. You can buy a nice cloth coat and pin money to it," Barker says.

The antifur campaign appears to be very successful. Fur sales from 1988 to 1989 did not increase. Several furriers have announced that they are going out of business. Antifur activists in Vail, Colorado, got a proposition on the ballot in 1989 banning the sale of furs. Although it did not pass, the proposition attracted national attention.

While it is unlikely that all fur ranching will end, there are compromises that may be reached in the treatment of fur-bearing animals. Many people propose setting standards for cage size and cleanliness. These standards could be set and enforced by state licensing boards or the Animal Welfare Act. Also, more humane ways of killing these animals could be developed. Some unreliable methods, such as electrocution, could be abandoned for more humane

Animal rights activists want to put a stop to the killing of animals for fur. Here, a trapper kills a coyote for its pelt.

About four thousand animal rights activists hold a protest march during the Christmas shopping season. It takes approximately fifty animals to make just one fur coat.

methods, such as gassing. The examination of this issue has prompted people to discuss the value and morality of fur products.

Puppy farms

Americans spend more than $500 million a year on pedigreed puppies purchased at pet stores, swap meets, and dog and gun shows. According to Robert Baker, chief investigator for the Humane Society, more than half a million of these puppies come from puppy mills.

A puppy mill is a breeding operation that mass-produces pedigreed animals for sale to animal dealers and pet stores. Unlike legitimate breeders who maintain a small number of animals and try to find good homes for their puppies, puppy mill breeders regard dogs only as a product to sell.

There are five thousand puppy mills in the United States, most of them in the Midwest states of Kansas, Missouri, Nebraska, Oklahoma, Iowa, and Arkansas. A large puppy mill contains as many as 500 dogs, with each female dog producing up to 20 pups a year. Registered kennel owners breed their dogs no more than once a year, producing an average of 5 pups a litter. Some puppy mills reportedly sell 120,000 puppies annually.

Ignorance of proper breeding practices

Most of those who run puppy mills are small farmers trying to supplement their income, according to Robert Baker. "A big problem with these people is that they are unaware of normal husbandry practices for dogs," he says. "They try to raise them like they would chickens, in double tiers of wire-bottomed cages that allow feces to fall to the ground." In these unsanitary conditions, the dogs become sick and infested with fleas and other parasites. "Puppy mill breeders buy standard-grade dog food for nursing mothers. That food would be all right for a pet dog, but a breeding mother needs extra nutrition," Baker added.

At a puppy mill, a female dog is bred at her first heat and every six months afterward until she can no longer breed, which happens when she reaches about five years of age. "Many breeders routinely destroy five-year-olds," according to Baker. Others take dogs that can no longer be used for breeding to an animal shelter.

Although federal regulations forbid shipping dogs before they are eight weeks old, puppy mills take puppies from their mothers at as young as four weeks. This saves the breeder the expense of extra dog food and puts the puppies in the pet store at an age when customers find them most appealing. The puppies are sold to dealers for between $50 and $150 each, depending on their breed. Dealers transport the puppies to the pet stores, where they may sell for as much as $1,500. According to Humane Society estimates, between 20 and 30 percent of the puppies die before they reach the pet store.

More than half a million of the puppies sold in pet stores, swap meets, and dog shows come from puppy mills. Many of these puppies end up in homes with children.

Purchasers of dogs from puppy mills may get more than they bargained for. Baker says that the inbreeding that occurs at the mills often causes congenital, or birth-related, deformities that may not show up for years. Sue Steinberg, an animal services worker with the ASPCA, reports that such dogs often have bad temperaments. "We see a lot of pet store-quality dogs given up to the ASPCA because of aggression, fearfulness, shyness, and the inability to be trained," she says. "These [qualities] are all passed through inbreeding."

Steve Poore, legislative and public affairs spokesperson for the USDA, says, "What we're hoping is to get puppy mill owners into compliance [with the law]." The USDA which is responsible for enforcing the Animal Welfare Act has set up a new animal welfare division and requested a larger budget to do the job.

Enforcement and prevention

Local and state animal welfare laws are on the books that might help close down the puppy mills, but they are seldom enforced. Baker knows of only two cases that have ever gone to court. In 1989, one puppy mill he investigated turned out to belong to the county sheriff. "Puppy mills are located in rural areas, where there's not a lot of sympathy for animal abuse," he says. Authorities usually just warn violators to clean up their operation.

California, a state that has virtually no puppy mills, is the largest buyer from breeding farms. About 300,000 puppies a year—60 percent of all the puppies sold in California—are imported from the Midwest. In 1988, legislators passed a law intended to boycott puppy mills. The law bans the importation of puppies less than twelve weeks.

What is the solution to the problem of puppy mills? The ASPCA recommends adopting a dog (or cat) from your local humane society instead of a

In some countries, dogs are used for meat. Here, dogs are packed into small cages awaiting shipment to markets.

store that gets its stock from mills. Another solution is to buy from a recognized breeder in your area so that you can see the animal's parents and their living conditions.

Finally it seems likely that puppy mills will be more rigorously inspected now that the USDA has received additional funding. The American Kennel Club (AKC), which registers pedigreed dogs in the United States, would be a logical choice to take steps that would close down many puppy mills. The Cat Fanciers' Association, a similar group that registers cats, has set rules for cat breeding operations that include standards for cage size and design. Breeders who violate these rules are not allowed to register their kittens with the association. If the AKC enacted rules setting minimum standards for kennels, the puppy mills would be forced to conform or lose their privilege of registering dogs.

6

Animals in the Wild

HUNTING IS ONE of the oldest organized activities of humans and dates back 500,000 years to the first hunting-gathering cultures. Even in modern times, isolated tribes like the Inuit in Canada and Alaska have followed this way of life, obtaining their food by hunting wild animals and gathering wild fruits and vegetables. Such cultures have existed in every part of the globe.

Today, however, relatively few people hunt for survival. Hunting has become instead a sport, a pastime enjoyed by nearly sixteen million Americans. Seven percent of the U.S. population purchased hunting licenses in 1989.

If hunting is no longer necessary for survival, why do so many people continue to hunt? Hunters like Charley Reese say the whole experience of being in the wild is important to them. "The hunter actually enjoys the outdoors," he says. "The hunter sleeps on the ground, cooks over a campfire or camp stove, gets up before dawn and spends hours and hours absorbed in the beauty of nature's wonders."

President George Bush, who has been a hunter for twenty-five years, says he likes hunting with friends. "When you are walking out in a field and the quail

(opposite page) This Wisconsin teenager went hunting for deer and came back with a 635-pound black bear. Some people hunt for food. Some for sport. Others hunt for trophies to place on their walls.

are fleshed [fly into the air as dogs or people approach them], there's just a physical thrill," he says. "It's the excitement factor, the outdoors, the love of nature, the beauty that's normally associated with [hunting], the relaxation, the camaraderie [shared companionship]. All these things come together."

Others, like Steve Judd, a student at Radford University in Virginia, say they value the traditions of hunting and the wilderness skills that they learn while hunting. "I don't care if I get a deer and neither do my friends," he insists. "Being outside, tramping the hedgerows on a crisp morning, that's as important as shooting something. Killing is only a tiny part of the overall experience."

Getting ready to hunt

Hunting is not simply a matter of walking out into the woods and shooting any animal you can find. Hunting is regulated by both state and federal

Deer hunters in Minnesota display their game. Game animals such as deer, bear, elk, and antelope may be hunted only in specified seasons.

laws and requires a great deal of preparation.

A hunter is allowed to kill only game animals and only at certain times. Game animals are those that are traditionally considered good for sport hunting. They usually include animals that are killed for food, such as duck, or for trophies, such as bighorn sheep. Federal and state wildlife officials set specific times of the year, called hunting seasons, when game may be taken. Game animals that may be hunted only in season include deer, bear, elk, antelope, buffalo, mountain lion, wild pig, bighorn sheep, squirrel, rabbit, turkey, pheasant, quail, partridge, dove, goose, and duck.

Restrictions

Becoming licensed to hunt is not simple. Most states require an applicant to complete a hunting safety course before receiving a hunting license, which is good for one year. Once in possession of a license, the hunter must still buy tags, or stamps, that permit the person to kill a limited number of game animals or birds. For example, in most states, each deer hunter is allowed to buy only two deer tags. He or she must put a tag on each deer killed. In this way, the states regulate the number of deer killed and obtain funds for wildlife programs.

Even after getting a license and the proper permits, the hunter must find a place to hunt. The demand is so great for hunting on public lands that states like California conduct a lottery to decide who wins the chance to hunt in choice locations. It is also possible to hunt at national wildlife refuges, on private property, or in private preserves. Several hunting clubs have been formed to assure their members access to game. Two of the largest of these include Ducks Unlimited, with a membership of 600,000, and Quail Unlimited, whose membership is 26,000.

No two hunts are exactly alike. Duck hunters often await the arrival of migrating flocks in a duck "blind," a hiding place arranged to camouflage their presence. They lure the birds to the water with duck calls—wooden devices that, in the hands of the skillful, sound like other ducks. Then, the hunters shoot at the landing ducks. Trained dogs, called retrievers, jump into the water and bring the ducks that have been shot to their masters.

Dogs are used in other kinds of hunting, too. Pointers stiffen into a pointing position when they locate a pheasant or grouse so that their masters can shoot the bird when it takes to the air. Tracking dogs smell the scent of a mountain lion, deer, or wild pig and help their masters follow its trail through the wilderness.

But in many cases, hunters do not rely upon the senses of a dog. They use their own tracking ability and knowledge of wildlife to find and kill their quarry with a rifle, crossbow, or other weapon. It is the responsibility of each hunter to track down and kill any animal that he or she might have wounded.

According to *U.S. News & World Report,* during the 1988-1989 hunting season, licensed American hunters killed 25 million rabbits, 4 million white-tailed deer, 50 million mourning doves, and 115,000 pronghorn antelope, along with numerous other species. In the same year, they spent $517 million on hunting licenses, duck stamps, and taxes on equipment and ammunition.

The right to hunt

For many Americans, hunting is a valued right dating back to colonial times. The first settlers on this continent had little hunting experience because in Europe and England, hunting was restricted to the aristocracy who owned most of the land. A person from the lower classes who was caught hunting faced severe punishment, sometimes even hanging. Common people were not allowed to own guns.

When they came to America, colonists enjoyed the freedom and self-sufficiency hunting gave them. Hunting became a part of American life.

Yet as more Americans move from the country to the city, the number of hunters decreases. The population of hunters declined by 700,000 between 1975 and 1990. Over 90 percent of the American people do not hunt. And the number of people photographing wildlife instead of shooting it has tripled in recent years.

A study by Professor Stephen Kellert of Yale University indicates that opposition to hunting among the nonhunting public is rising. While more than 80 percent of the Americans he surveyed approve of hunting to put meat on the table, 80 percent disapprove of

Some people say hunting is tragic and wasteful. Others say it is essential to maintain healthy animal populations in the wild. Here, two hunters return to camp with a deer.

hunting for trophies. Sixty percent feel that hunting just for recreation or sport is wrong, and one-third wants to ban hunting altogether.

Several animal rights groups, including the Humane Society, the Fund for Animals, and PETA (People for the Ethical Treatment of Animals), are campaigning to end hunting. In 1990 they succeeded in getting an initiative passed to ban trophy mountain lion hunting in California. They also were able to take court action to block bear hunting in New Jersey.

"We want to stigmatize hunting," says Wayne Pacelle, director of the Fund For Animals. "We see it as the next logical target [for the animal rights movement], and we believe it is vulnerable." Pacelle organized demonstrations during Connecticut's hunting season in 1989. Groups of animal activists followed hunters, harassing them and making loud noises to frighten the game.

Harassment has proven so successful at disrupting the hunt that hunters have asked state and federal lawmakers for help to stop it. Thirty-five states now have laws against harassing hunters. Similar laws are under discussion in most states, and Congress is considering proposals to ban this type of demonstration. Thirty states forbid driving animals away to protect them from hunters.

Special privileges for hunters

Such legislative protection of hunters' interests is not the only special treatment they receive, say animal rights activists. The activists point out that hunters often control the fish and game agencies that are supposed to conserve wildlife. For example, the Massachusetts Fisheries and Wildlife Board requires a majority of its seven-member commission to be hunters or trappers. Hunter-controlled agencies, activists say, concentrate on enhancing game populations by clearing brushland, damming streams, and killing predators. Often, other species suffer from these activities. "Having hunters oversee wildlife," says Pacelle, "is like having Dracula guard the blood bank."

Those who oppose hunting are especially angry that hunting and trapping are allowed in U.S. wildlife refuges. According to Lewis Regenstein, author of *The Politics of Extinction,* the U.S. Department of the Interior encourages or allows hunting on about half the refuges in the national wildlife refuge system. "This is done in spite of the fact that 96 percent of the visitors do not hunt, and about 85 percent of the money spent to maintain the refuges comes out of general tax funds, paid for by the American public," he says.

"Our refuges were established. . .to *safeguard* wildlife," says John Hoyt, president of the Humane Society. Hoyt believes that hunting violates the intent and purpose of wildlife refuges.

The importance of hunting

Hunters respond to these attacks by explaining that they contribute a great deal of money, which is

"Why don't they thin their own damned herd?"

used to preserve wildlife, in return for the right to hunt. Hunting is also an important part of the country's economy. Millions of dollars are spent each year on guns, clothing, and other equipment, and remote areas often depend on visiting hunters for much of their annual income. Finally, many hunting groups actively help wildlife populations in need. In the late 1980s, hunters provided food for starving elk in Yellowstone National Park and helped build watering troughs for sheep in the desert. "The hunter does more to conserve animals than anybody else," one hunter says.

An important part of conservation is wildlife management, the task of keeping populations of wild species in balance with their environment. According to wildlife management theory, responsible hunting helps control wildlife populations by reducing the number of surplus animals. Ecologists and conservationists believe that humans must help keep the animal population in balance. This is especially important since development and exploration have reduced the area where wild animals can live, disrupting habitats and killing many populations of natural predators. In the remaining wilderness areas, without natural predators, some species reproduce too rapidly, which causes them to fight for limited food and space.

Protecting the habitat

Each wildlife habitat has a carrying capacity, or the capability of supporting only so many animals. When too many animals live in one habitat, it is destroyed. Vegetation is killed off by overbrowsing, which exposes topsoil that washes away in the next rainfall. With the rich topsoil gone, new vegetation cannot establish itself.

As the habitat is destroyed, many animals starve or become ill. Disease spreads rapidly though the overcrowded habitat. It may even spread to nearby livestock and pets. "Hunting is a tool to control the population of wild animals," concludes Burt Ward, a member of the Safari Club.

Supporters of hunting include respected conservation organizations like the World Wildlife Fund, the Audubon Society, and the Sierra Club as well as state fish and game commissions. A policy statement of the Sierra Club says, "When necessary, acceptable management techniques such as. . .regulated periodic hunting. . .should be employed within natural as well as modified ecosystems to promote optimum [the best] diversity and numbers of wildlife."

One thing both activists and hunters agree upon is that it is a critical time for American wildlife. "At some point in the future, the public will look back and realize this was a pivotal juncture for saving our wild animals," says Joel Scrafford, a senior agent with the U.S. Fish and Wildlife Service in Montana.

The lack of natural predators

In preserves like Yellowstone National Park, a lack of predators has resulted in too many grass-eating animals. In 1989, overpopulation forced 569 buffalo out of park boundaries in search of food. Fearful that the buffalo would infect livestock with

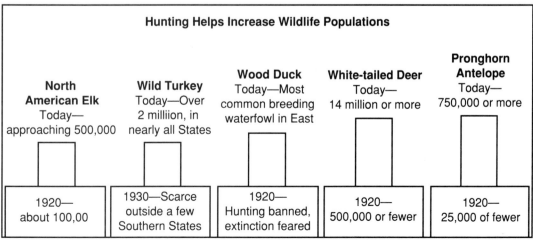

Hunting Helps Increase Wildlife Populations

North American Elk Today— approaching 500,000	Wild Turkey Today—Over 2 milliion, in nearly all States	Wood Duck Today—Most common breeding waterfowl in East	White-tailed Deer Today— 14 million or more	Pronghorn Antelope Today— 750,000 or more
1920— about 100,00	1930—Scarce outside a few Southern States	1920— Hunting banned, extinction feared	1920— 500,000 or fewer	1920— 25,000 of fewer

SOURCE: U.S. Department of Interior, Fish and Wildlife Service, *50 Years of Restoring America's Wildlife, 1937-1982.*

Montana officials authorized a buffalo hunt in Yellowstone National Park when overpopulation threatened the health of nearby cattle. Here, hunters look over their kill.

brucellosis, a disease that does not harm buffaloes but is lethal to cattle, Montana officials authorized a buffalo hunt.

Television coverage of hunters shooting unresisting buffalo from distances as close as six feet while demonstrators screamed and cried aroused the emotions of millions of viewers. Even hunters objected to the slaughterhouse atmosphere. "It resulted in bad press," says one National Rifle Association representative. "People in big cities didn't like it, and I understand their feelings."

Wildlife experts believe that scenes such as the buffalo hunt need not happen if the buffalo's natural predator, the wolf, is reintroduced into the park. However, the wolf's undeserved reputation as a killer of humans and the ranchers' natural concern for their livestock have so far blocked this plan.

Although management programs have ensured that species like the white-tailed deer, pheasant, and quail are still plentiful in the United States, other game populations are declining. Most species of ducks are suffering from the loss of wetland habitat in their breeding and wintering areas. According to *U.S. News & World Report,* the fall 1989 migratory flight numbered only 64 million birds, the second smallest on record. Before the decline began in 1980, annual flights averaged 91.5 million ducks. Black bear, antelope, and bighorn sheep are also disappearing from their ranges. Animal rights advocates believe that stopping hunting would allow these species to recover.

Hunting to control wildlife numbers

Pro-hunting advocates respond that now would be the worst time to ban the sport. They argue that without money generated from hunting less would be available for conservation effort. "If you eliminate [hunters], you lose the greatest source of conservation revenue," says John Turner, head of the

U.S. Fish and Wildlife Service.

The American Humane Association (AHA) does not support using hunters in to reduce surplus populations of wild animals. The AHA claims that sport hunting is not efficient. For example, in a 1987 hunt in New York, thirty-four deer were killed, but another thirty-three deer were wounded. Bow-and-arrow hunters are even less likely to kill an animal they shoot. Studies in Texas over a fifteen year period confirm the inefficiency of bow-and-arrow hunting. While Texas hunters using rifles and other guns retrieve 90 percent of the deer they shoot, bow-and-arrow hunters find only 50 percent of the deer they hit.

"It is impossible to ascertain the amount of pain and suffering hunters cause the countless millions of animals each year which are wounded and escape to die a slow and agonizing death," says author Lewis Regenstein. "Not to mention the millions of orphaned and crippled animals that fill the woods at the end of the hunting season."

Differing viewpoints about wildlife

This conflict is not limited to the issue of hunting. It reflects two different ways of looking at wildlife. On one side, animal rights supporters like the Humane Society, PETA, and the Fund for Animals are concerned with the lives of individual animals. They claim that animals suffer when they are killed by hunters or trappers.

These groups condemn current animal management programs because they involve killing some species to encourage the survival of others. In 1988, the U.S. Animal Damage Control program killed over 4.5 million mammals and birds to protect ranchers' livestock. Among the animals killed were 207 mountain lions, 291 black bears, and 1,163 bobcats, all animals whose numbers are declining nationally.

On the other side, hunters, trappers, and many wildlife authorities talk about the welfare of entire species. They see nothing wrong with killing individual animals for recreation or for economic or ecological reasons.

The Broken Arrow Archer Club of Minnesota says, "Hunting and trapping do not cause more suffering than naturally occurs to wild animals. People opposed to trapping and hunting would have you believe that wild animals and birds do not know pain and just fade away in death. . . . This is far from correct! Ninety percent of all animals in the wild die violently."

Those who support hunting consider wildlife a renewable resource, like timber, something that can be "harvested" again and again. According to this idea, species in the wild need to be kept in balance by hunting, trapping, and other measures to prevent widespread starvation and disease.

Harvesting wildlife

The controversy over harvesting wildlife is also at the heart of the fur trade debate. While most people seem to accept sport hunting as part of American life, commercial hunting and trapping does not enjoy such a positive public image. A large part of the American public is convinced that commercial hunting or trapping for furs is brutal and unnecessary.

The first successful campaign against harvesting wildlife began in 1969, when Brian Davies became disturbed by the slaughter of baby harp and hood seals for their white coats. Every year hunters bludgeoned, or hit to death more than 200,000 seals, using clubs. Most of these were babies on the ice floes off the coast of Canada. Davies founded the International Fund for Animal Welfare (IFAW) in 1969 after witnessing this bloody harvest of seals.

International publicity helped end the seal hunts

forever. Davies brought journalists to the seal hunt. Their reports and photos of hunters clubbing helpless, white-coated baby seals upset the public. In 1982, 3.5 million people signed petitions asking the European Economic Community (EEC) to ban the import of baby seal products. The EEC did ban baby seal products the next year. Closing the biggest market for baby sealskins led to the end of the hunt itself. This ban occurred in one of the few areas left in the world where hunters who live off the game they hunt still exist.

An unexpected result of the ban on baby sealskins was the collapse of the traditional Inuit Indian culture in the Canadian Arctic. Until the end of the 1970s, 90 percent of the Inuits made their living exclusively from selling sealskins. The Inuits never hunted the baby seals that caused the controversy because seals reach maturity before migrating to the Arctic. But after the ban on baby seal products took effect, consumers refused to buy *any* seal product. Today, most Inuits live on welfare because they can no longer support themselves.

Field and Stream columnist George Reiger contends that most trappers are similarly dependent on the fur trade. "There are still roughly 250,000 Americans who earn all or a significant portion of their livelihoods in the fur trade," he says. "Without trapping, thousands of men who take pride in providing for themselves and their families would be stripped of this dignity and forced to accept public

Seal hunters, shown here, try to stun their prey with blows to the head before the animals are skinned. But after hours of work, the hunters sometimes lose strength and accuracy and the seals remain conscious.

or private charity."

Although the seal hunts have been banned, trapping continues. Every year in the United States at least ten million animals are trapped for their fur. Most commonly trapped are raccoons, beavers, coyotes, lynx, minks, and foxes. However, birds, dogs, cats, deer, squirrels, and other animals also blunder into the traps. The Humane Society estimates that more than three million nontarget animals—called "trash animals" by trappers—are caught each year.

The Conibear trap

Animal advocates consider the use of leg-hold traps inhumane. They claim that hunters may wait many days before they return to check the traps and kill the animals. Those that escape by chewing off their trapped limbs may later die of loss of blood or infection. These same objections have convinced sixty countries and four states to outlaw the leg-hold trap. Some people want trappers to use the Conibear trap, developed in the 1940s by Frank Conibear, a Canadian trapper. This trap is designed to catch the animal by the neck or spine, killing it instantly. Conibear won an award from AHA for his trap.

Still, the Conibear trap does not work perfectly. Trappers do not like it because they say it does not always kill the animals it traps. "The Conibear seldom kills outright, and there is no possibility of an animal's body becoming numb, as would a foot in a foot-hold trap. Instead, the animals in a Conibear may struggle longer," says the Broken Arrow Archery Club.

Another problem is that a Conibear trap can kill dogs, and even small children that are accidentally caught. With a leg-hold trap, the most these accident victims might suffer is a broken leg or foot.

For these reasons, most animal rights and animal welfare organizations have concluded that there is no way of obtaining furs that does not involve ani-

This trapped raccoon is one of roughly ten million animals trapped for fur in the United States each year.

mal pain and suffering.

A booklet from Furbearers Unlimited, a pro-trapping group, proclaims:

> Unfortunately, most of [those who oppose trapping] have not had the opportunity to become acquainted firsthand with wild animals and their needs. These people have been influenced by fictional and often inaccurate films. In such films wild animals . . . are often humanized. They become cuddly, lovable little critters, often dressed in human clothes.
>
> Our fur resources, and our other renewable wildlife resources, are far too valuable to be lost on the basis of emotion, hearsay, and the unproven personal opinions of people who are not wildlife authorities in the problems of wild animals.
>
> In spite of anything you may have heard, modern trapping is necessary, humane, promotes conservation of both animals and their habitat, and provides supplemental income for thousands of people.

This quote illustrates what most trapping supporters believe. They point out that no fur-bearing animals in North America are endangered by the fur trade. They deny that trapping causes more suffering than naturally occurs to wild animals.

Most wild animals die violently. According to the Ohio Department of Natural Resources, "Death in nature is due to [attacks from predators], fighting, accident, starvation or disease. All of these can be considered, in human terms, cruel or inhumane. There is no moral justification for preferring the unobserved 'natural' death to the observed trapping death."

Trappers further protest that they are not uncaring monsters. Anyone who wants to be a trapper must undergo special training and must pass a test that includes knowledge of the animals themselves, the laws about trapping, and humane trapping methods. Ethical training is a part of the trapper educational program, which stresses humane treatment of the animals caught.

Debate over the future of wildlife

While it is uncertain which side will prevail in this debate over the future of wildlife, it is clear that the issue is expanding to include all wildlife. And it is receiving more attention from the animal rights movement. While protesters failed to stop the government hunt of buffalo that had strayed from Yellowstone National Park onto neighboring ranch land, other hunts have been canceled or reduced because of the campaign. California's 1990 bow-and-arrow hunting season was called off after protests, and dove hunting was blocked in Michigan and New York.

These protests reflect a changing awareness of wild animals. The days when wildlife in the United States numbered in the untold millions are over. Few people would disagree that steps must be taken to preserve what remains. The question being decided today is what is the best way to do it.

Some people consider leg-hold traps inhumane. Some animals chew off their trapped limbs to escape and then die from loss of blood or infection.

7

What You Can Do

WHAT CAN YOU do to protect animals? This simple question, like so many in the animal rights controversy, has no simple answer. Even the most knowledgeable animal lovers differ over what to do.

It is not necessary to agree with all the claims of animal rights activists to believe that animals deserve better treatment. Nor do you have to join a demonstration to express your support for animal rights. There are many ways you can help animals, from volunteering at the animal shelter to becoming aware of the ingredients in the products you use.

Pets

Animal rights begin at home. There are an estimated 100 million cats and dogs kept as pets in the United States. Other popular pets include birds, hamsters, gerbils, mice, and rats. While many people love and care for their animal companions, not every animal has a loving home.

The first thing you can do in the fight for animal rights is to set a good example in how you care for your pets. Make sure your dog or cat is neutered or spayed; wears a collar with proper identification attached to it; and is routinely vaccinated, regularly exercised, fed a balanced diet, and adequately shel-

(opposite page) These puppies are just two of thousands that end up in animal shelters every year.

109

People who feel strongly about an issue sometimes join organizations that share their concerns, as did these people who are protesting the use of animals for medical research.

tered. Never let your pet run loose unsupervised.

If you are thinking about getting a pet, it is wise to consider the matter carefully. Are you ready to provide a loving home for this animal for its full lifetime? Dogs and cats can live to be twenty years old, if well cared for. Have your parents agreed? Young people sometimes fall in love with a cute baby animal and bring it home, only to find that their parents have very good reasons why they cannot keep it. Finally, who will care for the new pet and pay for its food and veterinary care? You should reach an agreement on these questions with other family members before you bring home that cuddly puppy, playful kitten, or exotic snake.

If for some reason you are unable to keep your pet, try to find it a good home. Careful screening of prospects will help you choose the right person and insure that your pet will still be in a happy home years later. Do not be afraid to ask questions, make rules, or say no to someone.

If you cannot find someone to adopt your pet, take it to an animal shelter. Shelter workers try very hard to find a home for every animal. If a suitable owner is not found, your pet will be euthanatized.

Some animal owners, knowing that their pets run the risk of being put to sleep if they turn them over to shelters, abandon them instead. Most of these abandoned animals die of starvation, illness, or injury. A quick, peaceful death by injection is a kindness you owe an animal you can no longer care for.

Report animal cruelty

You can help enforce existing anticruelty laws by taking action when you witness animal cruelty and neglect. Talk to the person responsible for the abuse or neglect *only* if you think it is safe to do so. Humane Society officials say that such people will sometimes attack those who try to stop them and often treat the animal more harshly when someone tries

These kittens, found in a dumpster, provide an example of what not to do with unwanted animals. In most cities and towns, animal shelters or the local humane society can help with unwanted animals.

to interfere. If you are at school, notify a teacher or other authority. If you are elsewhere, get help from an adult. Call the local animal welfare organization or animal control officer when you know of animals that are injured or severely mistreated.

There are a number of groups you can contact if this does not solve the problem. Notify local or national dog, cat, or horse breeders' clubs if the matter involves pedigreed animals. Speak to animal control authorities or the local prosecutor, sometimes called the district attorney or state's attorney, when laws are being broken.

Keep good records. Write down the date, time, and address as well as names and descriptions of the people and animals involved in an incident of neglect or cruelty. With this information, the authorities will be able to press charges.

There are many types of cruelty to animals, and every state has its own laws dealing with them. Some states simply forbid any kind of "inhumane" or "needlessly cruel" treatment of animals. Others have both a general ban on cruel treatment and specific laws prohibiting certain activities that are considered cruel, such as organizing fights between animals. But even states that do not have a specific law against some form of cruelty can prosecute offenders under the general law.

For example, the Texas anticruelty law given be-

Many people believe that keeping animals locked up in cages is cruel and unnecessary.

low covers nearly every kind of mistreatment of animals. A person in Texas commits an offense if he or she intentionally or knowingly:

This woman volunteers her time at the San Francisco Society for the Prevention of Cruelty to Animals.

(1) tortures or seriously overworks an animal;
(2) fails unreasonably to provide necessary food, care, or shelter for an animal in his or her custody;
(3) abandons unreasonably an animal in his custody;
(4) transports or confines an animal in a cruel manner;
(5) kills, injures, or administers poison to an animal, other than cattle, horses, sheep, swine, or goats, belonging to another without legal authority or the owner's effective consent;
(6) causes one animal to fight with another; or
(7) uses a live animal as a lure in dog race training or in dog coursing on a racetrack.

When authorities bring formal charges of neglect or mistreatment against an owner, the animal involved is usually taken away from the owner after a hearing. In cases of severe mistreatment, the animal

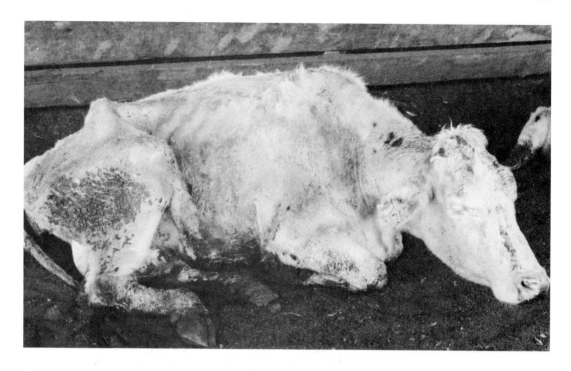

Cruel behavior toward animals can be reported to various people, including local animal control officials. Here, an emaciated calf rests.

is taken away immediately. Those convicted of animal abuse may be fined or even imprisoned.

Make a difference

One person can make a difference in the way animals are treated. The following activities were suggested by several animal rights and animal welfare groups, including PETA, the Animal Protection Institute of America, and the Humane Society.

1. You can join an animal welfare or animal rights organization. It will keep you informed of important national and international issues.

2. You should know your state's wildlife code and animal regulations and you should report any violations promptly. For information about, or copies of, state and federal animal protection laws, ask your local library or animal shelter.

3. Become a member of a local humane society or animal shelter. Many humane organizations have special clubs for young people.

4. You can become more knowledgeable yourself and educate others by researching animal topics for reports or classroom discussions. Many of the organizations listed at the back of this book will be happy to supply information on pet care, endangered species, animal rights, or other topics.

5. Read newspapers and magazines for articles about animals or animal abuse. Write letters of complaint or praise to organizations or companies mentioned in a story. If your complaints get no response, write to local government officials. Send a copy of the clipping to a national animal welfare organization, such as the Animal Protection Institute of America, for its information and possible action.

6. Write letters to local and state officials, members of Congress, and heads of state and federal agencies supporting strong animal welfare laws.

7. Encourage clubs to sponsor animal or ecology-related projects. Possibilities include talks by humane society officers or wildlife agency officials, trips to wildlife preserves, and obtaining permission to plant special food and cover plants for wildlife in

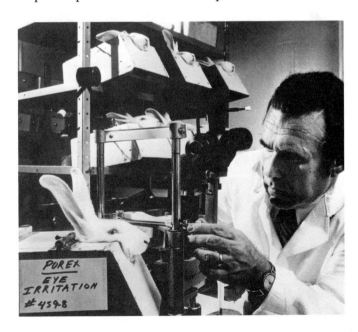

Consumers who feel strongly about animal testing for household products, such as the Draize test on rabbits, can write to the manufacturer about their concerns.

a local park.

8. Use your power as a consumer. Get and follow a shopper's guide to products made without animal testing. Write to companies that test their products on animals to express your opinions. Information on "cruelty free" products and companies that use animal testing is available from the Animal Protection Institute of America, Beauty Without Cruelty, the Humane Society, and the National Anti-Vivisection Society.

9. Be aware of what you eat. Range-fed beef and chicken are available from farmers' cooperatives, and some commercial companies like Zacky Farms claim that their poultry is humanely raised. Health food stores and local farmers often sell eggs from hens that are not kept in battery cages.

10. Do not buy pets from a large retail store. You can find purebreds as well as mixed breeds at the local animal shelter. If you have your heart set on a

Many wonderful pets, like this dog, can be found in animal shelters.

particular breed of dog or cat, visit local kennels or catteries where you can see both parents and the conditions the animal was raised in.

11. Choose your wardrobe with animals in mind. Do not wear wild animal furs or duck or goose down. Avoid accessories and garments made of animal products such as butterflies, feathers, skins, ivory, and tortoiseshell.

Regardless of how you choose to become involved in protecting animals, you will find it a rewarding experience. You will learn more about animals and develop a more meaningful relationship with the pets in your life, while meeting many people who share your concerns. You will also be doing something you can be proud of—defending creatures that cannot defend themselves.

Glossary

anesthesia: A condition in which one feels no sensation of pain.

antivivisectionist: A person who is opposed to operating on or experimenting with living animals.

biomedical: Refers to a combination of medical, biological, and physical sciences. Biomedical research often studies how humans or animals cope with stressful situations, such as injury or illness.

cannibalism: Animals eating other animals of the same species, or humans eating other humans.

dissection: Cutting up animal or human bodies for scientific research.

evolution: The development of all species of plants and animals from earlier forms of life through slight changes inherited from preceding generations.

exploitation: Making use of someone or something in a way that is to the user's advantage.

game: Animals and birds that are usually hunted, such as deer, pheasant, duck, or turkey.

humane: Kind, tender, merciful, or considerate.

humanitarian: A person who tries to improve conditions for others.

husbandry: The care and raising of animals.

livestock: Farm animals, such as horses, cattle, and pigs.

molt: To shed feathers before growing new ones.

neuter: To remove the testicles of a male animal so that it cannot reproduce.

physiology: The study of human and animal bodies and how they operate.

spay: To remove the ovaries and uterus of a female animal so it cannot reproduce.

speciesism: A bias, like racism or sexism, that causes a person to automatically view animals as worth less than people.

vivisection: Operating or experimenting on living animals to observe biological processes.

118

Organizations to Contact

The following organizations are concerned with the issues covered in this book. All of them have publications or information available for interested readers.

Alliance for Animals
P.O. Box 909
Boston, MA 02103

Alternatives to Animals
P.O. Box 7177
San Jose, CA 95150

American Anti-Vivisection Society
801 Old York Road, Suite 204
Jenkintown, PA 19046

American Fund for Alternatives to Animal Research (AFAAR)
175 W. 12th St., Suite 16 G
New York, NY 10011

American Humane Association
Los Angeles Regional Office
14144 Ventura Blvd., Suite 260
Los Angeles, CA 91423

American Society for the Prevention of Cruelty to Animals (ASPCA)
441 E. 92nd St.
New York, NY 10128

Animal Allies
P.O. Box 35063
Los Angeles, CA 90035

Animal Legal Defense Fund
1363 Lincoln Ave.
San Rafael, CA 94901

Animal Liberation Front Support Group
1543 E St., #44
San Bernardino, CA 92405

Animal Liberation Network
P.O. Box 983
Hunt Valley, MD 21030

Animal Protection Institute of America
2831 Fruitridge Road
P.O. Box 22505
Sacramento, CA 95822

Animal Rights Action Group
P.O. Box 8087
Santa Cruz, CA 95061

Animal Rights Direct Action Coalition
P.O. Box 162335
Sacramento, CA 95816

The Animals' Voice Magazine
P.O. Box 34347
Los Angeles, CA 90034

Animal Welfare Institute
P.O. Box 3650
Washington, DC 20007

Argus Archives
228 E. 49th St.
New York, NY 10017

Beauty Without Cruelty
175 W. 12th St.
New York, NY 10012

Coalition to Abolish Classroom Dissection
P.O. Box 214, Planetarium Station
New York, NY 10024

Coalition to Abolish the LD50 and Draize Tests
P.O. Box 214, Planetarium Station
New York, NY 10024

Committee for Humane Legislation
1506 19th St. NW
Washington, DC 20036

Committee to Abolish Sport Hunting
P.O. Box 43
White Plains, NY 10605

Farm Animal Reform Movement
P.O. Box 70123
Washington, DC 20088

Friends of Animals
P.O. Box 1244
Norwalk, CT 06856

The Fund for Animals
200 W. 57th St.
New York, NY 10019

Furbearers Unlimited
P.O. Box 199
Wapella, IL 61777

Greenpeace
1611 Connecticut Ave. NW
Washington, DC 20009

Humane Farming Association
1550 California St., Suite 6
San Francisco, CA 94109

Humane Society of the United States
2100 L St. NW
Washington, DC 20037

In Defense of Animals
21 Tamal Vista Blvd.
Corte Madera, CA 94925

The Interfaith Council for the Protection of Animals and Nature
2913 Woodstock Ave.
Silver Spring, MD 20910

International Primate Protection League
P.O. Box 766
Summerville, SC 29484

New England Anti-Vivisection Society
333 Washington St., Suite 850
Boston, MA 02108-5100

People for the Ethical Treatment of Animals (PETA)
P.O. Box 42516
Washington, DC 20015

Performing Animal Welfare Society
P.O. Box 842
Galt, CA 95632

Pets Plus International
P.O. Box 7532
Olympia, WA 98507

Physicians Committee for Responsible Medicine
P.O. Box 63222
Washington, DC 20015

Primarily Primates
P.O. Box 15306
San Antonio, TX 78212-8506

Professional Rodeo Cowboys Association
101 Pro Rodeo Drive
Colorado Springs, CO 80919

Student Action Corps for Animals
P.O. Box 15588
Washington, DC 20003-0588

Students Against Dissection Hotline
1-800-FROG

Trans-species Unlimited
P.O. Box 1553
Williamsport, PA 17703

U.S. Fish and Wildlife Service
Publication Unit
18th & C Sts. NW
Washington, DC 20240

Suggestions for Further Reading

NON-FICTION

Miles Banton, *Animal Rights*. New York: Gloucester Press, 1987.

Patricia Curtis, *Animal Rights: Stories of People Who Defend the Rights of Animals*. New York: Macmillan Press, 1984.

Edward F. Dolan Jr., *Animal Rights*. New York: Franklin Watts, 1986.

Janelle Rohr, ed., *Animal Rights: Opposing Viewpoints*. San Diego: Greenhaven Press, 1989.

Peter Singer, *Animal Liberation: A New Ethics for Our Treatment of Animals*. New York: Avon Books, 1977.

The Animal Shelter. New York: Lodestar Books, 1984.

FICTION

Richard Adams, *Plague Dogs*. New York: Alfred A. Knopf, 1978.

Sterling North, *Rascal*. New York: E.P. Dutton, 1963.

Robert O'Brien, *The Secret of NIMH*. New York: Scholastic Books, 1982.

Marjorie Rawlings, *The Yearling*. New York: Charles Scribner and Sons, 1970.

Anna Sewell, *Black Beauty*. New York: Putnam Publishing Group, 1981.

Works Consulted

B.R. Boyd, *The New Abolitionists: Animal Rights and Human Liberation*. San Francisco: Taterhill Press, 1982.

Michael Allen Fox, *The Case for Animal Experimentation*. Berkeley: University of California Press, 1986.

J.J. McCoy, *In Defense of Animals*. New York: Seabury Press, 1978.

Tom Regan, *The Case for Animal Rights*. Berkeley: University of California Press, 1983.

Bernard E. Rollin, *Animal Rights and Human Morality*. Buffalo, New York: Prometheus Books, 1981.

Bernard E. Rollin, *The Unheeded Cry: The Testament of Animals in Scientific Research*. London: Oxford University Press, 1985.

George K. Russel, *Vivisection and the True Aims of Education in Biology*. 3rd ed. New York: Myer Institute, 1988.

Index

About the Author

Sunni Bloyd's love of animals began early. Growing up within roaring distance of the Sacramento Zoo, she brought home field mice trapped in her lunchbox and once kept a five-foot-long sand shark in the bathtub for a week. She filled the house with a menagerie of interesting creatures: cats, dogs, hamsters, parakeets, ducks, fish, snakes, butterflies, and even silkworms. Luckily, her mother (who had herself owned a pair of bearcubs as childhood pets) was understanding.

Bloyd earned a B.A. from the University of California at Davis, and a Master's Degree in Education at the University of Dayton in Ohio.

For many years a junior-high-school reading teacher, Bloyd now is an award-winning, full-time writer. She, her husband, and their two teen-aged sons live in Southern California with only a few cats, two rats, and an old dog.

Picture Credits

DATE DUE

1 Ju '93			
27 MY '94			
11 My '95			
DE 19 '96			
MR 26 '97			
AP 24 '97			
MY 22 '97			
2 Ju '97			
2 Ju '97			
MY 15 '00			
OC 16 '01			